MALVERN GIRLS' COLLEGE
A Centenary History

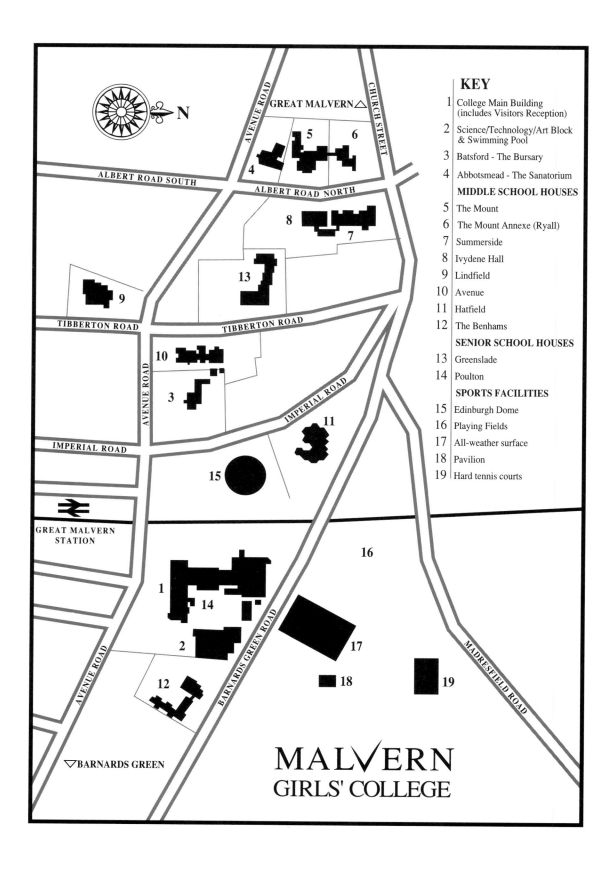

N

GREAT MALVERN △

KEY

1 College Main Building
(includes Visitors Reception)
2 Science/Technology/Art Block
& Swimming Pool
3 Batsford - The Bursary
4 Abbotsmead - The Sanatorium

MIDDLE SCHOOL HOUSES

5 The Mount
6 The Mount Annexe (Ryall)
7 Summerside
8 Ivydene Hall
9 Lindfield
10 Avenue
11 Hatfield
12 The Benhams

SENIOR SCHOOL HOUSES

13 Greenslade
14 Poulton

SPORTS FACILITIES

15 Edinburgh Dome
16 Playing Fields
17 All-weather surface
18 Pavilion
19 Hard tennis courts

AVENUE ROAD

CHURCH STREET

ALBERT ROAD SOUTH

ALBERT ROAD NORTH

TIBBERTON ROAD

TIBBERTON ROAD

AVENUE ROAD

IMPERIAL ROAD

IMPERIAL ROAD

GREAT MALVERN STATION

BARNARDS GREEN ROAD

MADRESFIELD ROAD

AVENUE ROAD

▽BARNARDS GREEN

MALVERN
GIRLS' COLLEGE

MALVERN GIRLS' COLLEGE
A Centenary History

Pamela Hurle

Pamela Hurle

Phillimore

1993

Published by
PHILLIMORE & CO. LTD.
Shopwyke Manor Barn, Chichester, Sussex

ISBN 0 85033 853 0

Printed and bound in Great Britain by
BIDDLES LTD.
Guildford, Surrey

Contents

List of Illustrations

Introduction and Acknowledgements

It is an honour to be asked to write the centenary history of one of the finest schools in the country but it is also a daunting responsibility. Inevitably some readers will be disappointed that someone or something very special to them is not even mentioned: I am sorry for this but hope that they will understand that one short book cannot embrace all that is precious to so many people. In trying to encapsulate the essence of the written records and the very personal comments of a wide range of people, I hope to have produced a book that is not just accurate but enjoyable—breaking from the old-fashioned mould of school histories with their tedious, dutiful recording of minutiae.

So many people have given invaluable help that it is very difficult to name them all. Sometimes a casual remark in a half-forgotten conversation has lodged in my mind and may appear in some comment in these pages—for this is a book written not simply to reminisce about the past but to ask questions about how and why this school became so important.

Special thanks are due to a large number of people whose contributions have given me particular pleasure. With the help of my colleague, Sylvia Harding, and Patricia Wilkinson, secretary of the Old Girls' Association, every member of that association was sent a questionnaire: the replies provided both helpful information and riveting reading—perhaps because total anonymity was promised to all who took the trouble to respond! At reunions old girls have chatted about their memories. The former secretary of the Old Girls' Association, Osra Garrish, during her long period in office carried out time-consuming and fascinating research which proved most useful. Barbara Chaning-Pearce, whose connections with the school span nearly 80 years, entertained and informed in her inimitable style. Peggy Edwards' written recollections of the school in the early 20th century form an invaluable archive which the school will always treasure. Miss Grace Phillips encouraged me to write this history, her own chronicle of the school under Miss Brooks being full of fascinating detail which helped me in my own task. Miss Burgess (headmistress 1954-68), Miss Mary Micklewright (on the staff from 1947 to 1973) and Marjorie Milne, whose memories covered a much earlier period, all offered me hospitality while I pestered them with questions. Miss Diana Medley, former school accountant, pointed me in the right direction for so many aspects of the school's history. Robin Hall, assistant bursar, has plied me with information as it has come to light. So, too, has Miss Therese Stockford, who fortunately did not retire from her long-held post as school registrar until 1992 so continued to feed me material until the book was almost ready for publication. Mrs. Rosemary Stanier, the school housekeeper, also rescued useful files from oblivion while Kenneth Lynes, who started to work at the school when he was a boy and now carries the heavy responsibilities of senior houseman, has retained his sense of humour and has a fund of stories to tell. Many colleagues have shared their memories with me as we sat in the staff-room: Mrs. Ivian Lloyd, housemistress of Summerside, has been especially helpful, as has Miss Patricia Drew, head of sixth form, who kept me afloat when I looked likely to drown in the welter of information and enquiry as to the progress of 'the book'.

Many people gave or lent material to add to the school's archives: much of it has been used in this book. Thanks for such generosity are due to Phyllis Castle, Kate Challis, Susannah Clasen, Pamela Cooper, Kenneth Davis, Mary Dixey, Peggy Edwards, Sally Forwood, Mary Kane, Erica Kidd, Vivienne MacKenzie, the *Malvern Gazette* and *Ledbury Reporter*, Mary Mills, Delmé Moore, Mrs Schmitt and Derryle Wynne. Much of the photographic material was very old and faded but the skill and patience of Jerry Mullaney have produced pictures which will, I think, give pleasure to many.

Several past and present members of the school community—all very busy people—spent precious free time reading my manuscript, occasionally urging me to think again about some aspect. This undoubtedly effected improvement but I take full responsibility for any remaining faults. These patient and knowledgeable readers were Mr. John Frith (Chairman of the school's governing Council), Miss Julia Hick (school librarian), Mr. Declan O'Neill (school development director), Air Commodore Brian Opie (school bursar and archivist), Miss Veronica Owen (headmistress from 1968 until 1983) and Dr. Valerie Payne (present headmistress). My husband, who has seen me through so many publications, deserves special tribute: without his encouragement and practical help none of my books would have been written.

PAMELA HURLE
January 1993

Chapter One

The Local and National Backcloth

How did this school become one of the top ten independent schools in the country? To appreciate the history of Malvern Girls' College it is necessary to understand the context in which it grew from very modest beginnings in 1893. This means that we must start by examining two subjects—the growth of Malvern and the state of girls' education in the 19th century.

Until the mid-19th century Malvern was an obscure little village, too far west to attract much attention in those times of poor communication and difficult roads. The priories at Great Malvern and Little Malvern, founded in the 11th and 12th centuries, were dissolved by Henry VIII in the sixteenth. Their foundation by monks, whose aim was to turn their backs upon the world and its temptations, indicates the obscurity of the region at the time of their foundation. Not much changed in the succeeding centuries, so neither they, nor the area, achieved any great fame or notoriety. True, there had been since Tudor times—possibly earlier—a modest fame for Malvern water which flowed from springs on the hills and was reputed to have a beneficial effect in the treatment of a variety of ills. But Malvern remained a village and never really exploited its water until the 18th and, more especially, the 19th centuries. In the 1750s Dr. John Wall, a man of diverse talents who helped to establish the famous porcelain factory at Worcester, analysed Malvern water and proved why it was so different from most other water—it was exceptionally free from impurity:

> The Malvern water, says Dr. John Wall
> Is famed for containing just nothing at all.

So it is clear that the springs of Malvern differed markedly from those at other spa towns whose claim to fame rested on the mineral content of their waters. But Malvern remained low in the league table of spa towns until the 1840s when two doctors came to transform the little village into an English equivalent of the flourishing spa at Graefenberg, the Bavarian town where Vincent Priessnitz had earned a world-wide reputation for his hydropathic work. Dr. James Wilson and Dr. James Manby Gully came to Malvern in 1842 dissatisfied with the standard medical practices of their day and full of enthusiasm for the use of pure water, externally and internally, for innumerable medical purposes. Malvern was never quite the same after their arrival. The doctors themselves set up hydropathic establishments and their success soon attracted others of their profession to come to Malvern and jump on the lucrative bandwagon of the water-cure. Local inhabitants increasingly earned their livelihoods from the health-conscious visitors who came to use Malvern water and listen to the pronouncements of the doctors.

Important features of hydropathy were a good plain diet, plenty of fresh air and vast quantities of Malvern water, preferably drunk straight from the springs on the hills. The doctors were astute businessmen who recognised the commercial potential of a source of pure water combined with the obsession of the self-indulgent with their health. Their recipe for

1

PRINCIPAL FRONT.

1 & 2.   Two views of the *Imperial Hotel*, opened in 1862. The garden front shows the view from Barnard's Green Road.

GARDEN FRONT,

good health was to enrich the doctors and countless others in Malvern. Boarding-houses and hotels began to proliferate, several of them making special arrangements for their guests to receive hydropathic treatment. The regime prescribed by the doctors was in stark contrast to the usual life-style of the affluent who could afford to come to Malvern: it is hardly surprising that, denied their usual intake of food and alcohol, so many felt fitter than they had done in years. As their health improved, so did Malvern's wealth.

Against this background, one of the grandest hotels in Worcestershire was opened in Malvern in 1862. Built as part of a grand scheme designed by E. W. Elmslie, the *Imperial* served as an hotel for nearly sixty years. Long after the water-cure declined, its German born owner struggled to keep it going but eventually sold it in 1919 to the expanding Malvern Girls' College. To many people it simply is the Girls' College, but it had a story of its own—outlined in Chapter Four—before the girls took over.

Within twenty years of Dr. Wilson and Dr. Gully coming to Malvern the village had become a small town with its own local government board carrying through numerous reforms to provide cleansing, lighting and other services. Much power, however, still rested with Lady Emily Foley, the imperious lady of the manor of Malvern who resided in some state at Stoke Edith in Herefordshire, a few miles to the west of the Malvern Hills. She came regularly across the hills to Malvern to supervise her estates here: widowed in her prime in 1846, she spent the rest of the century (she died on New Year's Day, 1900) ruling her late husband's estates as a more or less benevolent despot. Aware of the duties of her class, she was also fully conscious of its rights, and was not a lady to allow those rights to be eroded. She was a most effective town planner in an era which knew nothing of 20th-century bureaucracy with its planning applications, restrictions—and follies. Her power was equal to that of any planning committee, and many would consider her taste superior to that of some of them. She kept central Malvern as an enclave for the middle classes. Large houses, often built of Malvern stone and surrounded by lawns, shrubberies and high stone walls, insulated their well-to-do owners from many of the less pleasant realities of life. Lesser mortals earned a living from serving both the resident middle classes and the visitors who flocked to Malvern in ever greater numbers after the completion of the railway in the 1860s. By this time the trains brought not only the comfortable visitors wishing to undergo the rigours of the water-cure, but also day trippers from industrial regions such as the Black Country. Such day trippers seeking a day in the fresh air of the Malverns caused Lady Foley some consternation: she made sure that most of them were put off the trains at Malvern Link in order to keep Great Malvern, as far as possible, unsullied.

Into this rarefied air of Malvern a new group had started to arrive from 1865. Young gentlemen were being packed off to one of the country's newest public schools and, although Malvern College experienced a variety of teething troubles, by the end of the century it was well established. Its early financial difficulties had been resolved, the sporting problems of a site on a hill side had been tackled by extensive levelling and an academic reputation was also in the making. Girls did not feature in public school life at all and perhaps this is the point at which we should examine the state of girls' education at the time that Miss Poulton and Miss Greenslade founded the school that was to become Malvern Girls' College.

In the 19th century women were very much second-class citizens, notwithstanding such shallow tokens of respect as gentlemen standing up when a lady entered the room. A lady might never soil her hands but a woman from the lower ranks of society never stopped working. No analysis of girls' education in the 19th century can be attempted without first recognising the rigid class structure which then existed and was reinforced by the teaching of the church:

3.   Emphasis on a wide variety of baths available at the hotel is understandable: Dr. Gully who had, with Dr. Wilson, brought the water-cure to Malvern, was chairman of the hotel's board of management.

> The rich man in his castle,
>   The poor man at his gate;
> God made them high or lowly
>   And ordered their estate.

For ladies the only acceptable career was marriage, which actually offered some individuals excellent prospects: presiding over a large household demanded considerable managerial skills. But if a lady failed to find a husband to keep her in the manner to which she had been brought up in her father's house, she faced the serious problem of keeping body and soul together in a climate of opinion which forbade her to engage in the sordid business of earning a living wage. Since the work of a governess was almost the only reasonably respectable occupation open to such ladies, many unhappily embarked upon a lifestyle for which they were usually unqualified and often wholly unsuited. Their charges, frequently indulged by weak or uncaring parents, might make the life of the governess a misery and too often derived no perceptible benefit from her possibly inadequate services. Indeed, one wonders why on earth governessing was regarded as respectable, offering as it did so little satisfaction to governess, pupil or employer. The lot of governesses and the evils of such private schools as existed for girls were vividly described by both Anne Brontë in *Agnes Grey* and her sister Charlotte in *Jane Eyre*. In short, young ladies grew up for most of the 19th century without intellectual discipline or stimulus, and the vicious circle of female ignorance and inability to earn an honourable living was kept in motion.

For working-class women, manual labour was an inevitable part of life. Married or not, they were obliged to work long hours for pitiable wages. With marriage came frequent, exhausting pregnancies and the hard labour of looking after the family. Unmarried women—and many married ones, too—worked in factories, on the land, in shops and in their own or other people's homes. Some were driven to augment low wages by providing sexual favours to total strangers or to male employers who saw no illogicality in holding two different standards of propriety—one for themselves and another for their womenfolk. Working-class women had neither time nor much desire for education since it could not be seen to lighten their heavy load of manual work or to offer better financial rewards than the work they did already: to be a woman was to be part of a vast pool of cheap labour.

So, for all classes, education for girls rated a very low priority. In truth, education for boys did not rate very high either until well into the 19th century, and the state contributed nothing until in 1833 the Whig government made the first state grant to education. This took the form of £20,000 allocated to two religious societies which, since the early years of the century, had been trying to instill some elementary facts—and a good deal of religious indoctrination—into the heads of some thousands of working-class boys and girls.

But the mid-19th century saw some changed thinking. By 1870 the state's half-hearted interest had blossomed into a conviction that the education of the young was a means of improving society; the matter was given added urgency by the extension of the parliamentary vote to thousands of working-class men so that there had arisen a need 'to educate our masters'. The first schools maintained entirely by public money were set up following Forster's Act of 1870 and education soon became compulsory for all. Working-class girls sat alongside their brothers in schools maintained by local school boards and learned the 'three Rs'—reading, 'riting and 'rithmetic. At least, they sat alongside them until about the age of eight but after that age, according to accepted education theory, 'separation becomes indispensably necessary'. This facilitated setting the girls to learning the traditional skills of their sex: needlework and 'housewifery' prepared them to become thrifty wives and mothers.

The rich had little to do with such schools, beyond sitting on the governing bodies which controlled them. They did not wish their own sons and daughters to mix with their social inferiors—'the great unwashed'—and so made different arrangements for the education of their own children. That of their sons was usually regarded as infinitely more important than that of their daughters, and contained a heavy content of Latin and Greek grammar. The girls, it was hoped, would find husbands: it was considered foolish to run the risk of frightening off a potential husband by filling a girl's head with knowledge that would be of little use to her and might cause the young man to feel intellectually inferior. It was a widely held belief that men had better brains and few girls chose to call this into question. Few men, of course, saw any reason to doubt its truth.

One who did was a well-known theologian, the Rev. Frederick Denison Maurice, who held various university posts. He recognised the desirability of providing professional training for governesses and was associated with the foundation, in Harley Street, of Queen's College, which was set up for this purpose in 1848. The next year Bedford College was established so that for the first time women had their own facilities to enable them to benefit from the teaching of the rather progressive London University, which was still in its infancy. Very soon two pioneering girls' schools—North London Collegiate in 1850 and Cheltenham Ladies' College in 1853—began to set the pattern for what was needed if the education of girls was to be taken seriously. Miss Frances Buss was headmistress of the former, while Miss Dorothea Beale took over Cheltenham in 1858. Although often portrayed as a formidable pair, both possessed considerable charm; their strength of purpose may have seemed unfashionably unfeminine for their social class at that time but, like Florence Nightingale in another field at the same time, they recognised the futility of being shrinking violets when there were battles to be fought.

They were helped by the fact that the mid-19th century was a period which witnessed a kind of renaissance in education. The curriculum which had been taught for generations to boys was being seen as irrelevant in a Britain whose prosperity, based on invention and industry, had made it the most powerful nation in the world. The Clarendon Commission of 1861 highlighted the shortcomings of the great public schools such as Eton and Rugby and, together with the proselytising of reforming headmasters like Arnold, Thring and Butler, led to the introduction of new subjects and ideals. The new thinking naturally spilled over into girls' education and some old endowments were reconstituted to permit their use for the education of girls as well as—or even instead of—boys. New girls' schools were founded with an emphasis on subjects similar to those taught in the reformed boys' public and grammar schools, and in 1872 the Girls' Public Day School Company (later Trust) was set up to provide, not just schools for girls, but *good* schools for girls. This was a very daunting task indeed, for it required destroying the deep-seated prejudice that girls' education was somehow less important than that of boys: the magnitude of the task is perceived when we realise that in some dark places it is an attitude which still exists more than a hundred years later.

This, then, is the local and national background to the foundation in 1893 of the school which was to become Malvern Girls' College.

Chapter Two

Establishing the School 1893-1919

Malvern's reputation as a centre for independent education is relatively recently established. Of the independent schools in existence in the 1990s only one—Malvern College—was purpose-built, while Malvern Girls' College, now secure in what was once a grand hotel, began very modestly in a private house in 1893.

At that time there was nothing in particular to distinguish this new little school from several other similar enterprises in the town. Isabel Greenslade had trained at the Bedford Kindergarten Training College and came to Malvern full of enthusiasm to practise one of the few professions then open to respectable middle-class women—teaching. By the autumn of 1893 she was able to hold her first classes in the drawing-room of Ivydene—not the present

4.   This photograph and that shown in plate 5 (overleaf) are the earliest known of the school, and are loaned by a relative of one of the first pupils. This one shows the boys, admitted until the turn of the century, with Miss Poulton and Miss Greenslade standing at the back, and was probably taken in the drawing room of the Poultons' house in College Road.

Ivydene Hall, but a house now known as Ivybank in College Road. It was the home of an architect, William Ford Poulton, and his wife. These first classes were attended by five boys as well as five girls, their ages ranging from the baby of the group, aged two years and ten months, to the eldest, who was eight years old. The young pupils all came from comfortable Malvern families who could afford the fees. Many years later, one of them recalled sitting at desks, each of which held four children. They learned geography by means of trays of sand used to illustrate terms such as mountain, island, river-bed and isthmus. Round the room a wide shelf held models of animals and birds of the world, designed to teach natural history and show the relative sizes of the various creatures.

The day started with prayers at 9.45, each child being required to learn a verse of scripture daily. Reading, writing and arithmetic filled the time until the mid-morning break which was then called lunch. After the lunch came drill—early physical education—or kindergarten games until noon. Older children came for an additional hour in the afternoon to work at nature study, French, art, history or literature. So much did they enjoy all these pastimes that, it was claimed, they clamoured to be allowed to come to school on Saturdays— and got what they wanted!

Mrs. Poulton, who had earlier kept a school of her own, had progressive ideas on education, but she died in January 1894, soon after Miss Greenslade began her classes. Her daughter, Lily Poulton, who had gained some teaching experience in her mother's school,

5.   This photograph, also possibly taken in the drawing room of the Poultons' house, shows the girls, mostly rather older than the boys, though Miss Greenslade seems to be holding a particularly young child.

6.   Left to right: Miss Greenslade, Miss Mitchell and Miss Poulton, the three co-principals from 1902.
Miss Poulton seemed to have a marked preference for being photographed so as to show her left profile.

showed great interest in the new enterprise. Possibly it was her business acumen which helped
to raise the number of pupils to a very respectable total of 21 within 12 months. Her particular
interest was art, but she did not really come into her own until the school started to take
boarders, enabling her to find scope for her mothering instincts. The first boarders are said to
have been the young children of missionaries.

By 1896 additional room was needed, so the little boys were removed to accommodation
next door at the Masonic Lodge. Many people then believed fervently in the necessity of
educating even small boys and girls separately, so such segregation continued to be practised
as yet more rooms were rented at Dalvey at the end of College Road. Great faith was shown
in 1899 when 'Montpellier', a school for the 'daughters of gentlemen', kept for some years
by a Mrs. Norton, was purchased for £3,800, together with an acre of ground, and renamed
Ivydene Hall. This was a considerable rise in the educational world for Miss Poulton and Miss
Greenslade. An illustrated survey of Malvern made in 1894 had made no mention of their
modest school, but contained some interesting details about Montpellier, described as an
'aristocratic establishment'. Mrs. Norton, 'while possessing a large amount of the necessary
governing power, is at the same time kindly to a degree which must react favourably on the
pupils under her charge.' The worthy Mrs. Norton was also 'particularly keen on the sanitary
arrangements' and took care to treat her pupils as young ladies 'so that they may be ready to
make their entrance into society immediately on leaving school.'

7 & 8.   Some quite early group photographs were taken in less formal surroundings in the garden.

9 & 10.   Ivydene Hall, previously known as Montpellier, was the first major purchase made by Miss Poulton and Miss Greenslade. It was soon found inadequate to accommodate the girls and their activities, so an extra storey was added, dramatically altering the appearance of the house, as shown by comparison of these two photographs.

11. Summerside and Ivydene Hall as shown in an early prospectus.

Miss Poulton and Miss Greenslade had made a wise purchase: the property, still one of Malvern Girls' College's middle school boarding houses, has been in the College's hands longer than any other still owned by it, and was for 20 years the nucleus of the school as it grew in size and reputation. At the time of its purchase the two founders were joined by Miss Blanche Eleanor Mitchell, who became a co-principal. A most attractive woman, rather younger than the other two, she was to become the much loved 'B.E.M.'.

The turn of the century saw another major decision: having been responsible for the elementary education of over 60 little boys in the period 1893-99, Miss Poulton and Miss Greenslade reluctantly decided to stop accepting boys. In fact, boys' names appeared on the school admission list for some years into the 20th century though it is clear that much more emphasis was placed on attracting girls—a most understandable attitude in view of the purchase of an established school for young ladies. It was probably in 1900 that a large extension, housing a gymnasium and studio, was built on to the side of the newly named Ivydene Hall. This is now the spacious dining room for that house. In 1903 the neighbouring house was bought and connected with Ivydene by a gallery: for some time known as School House, it has been for generations of girls their boarding house, Summerside.

The decision to buy Montpellier began something of a stranglehold on property in Albert Road North, as the successful ladies next turned their attention to property on the opposite side

80.   Miss Brooks and others planting a tree at Hinton in commemoration that she and the Senior School spent 1939-40 there.

The contents of fourteen buildings were being poured by packers, some skilled from Cox and Painter's and Pickford's, some from the Labour Exchange most emphatically not, into 91 railway vans and containers ...

Then the great trek began ... Miss Puttock and Miss Phillips set out with Oliver in the Hillman to Hinton House. Their arrival was funny; thinking that they were going to an empty house, they had on the journey down loaded the car with unwrapped goods such as kettles, until it looked like a tinker's caravan, only to be greeted with, 'The Earl will receive you in the Boudoir', and with shame they watched his valet and entourage bearing away the contents of the Hillman ... The Earl's furniture had to be labelled and stored, our preliminary blackout put up, quarters found in the village for mistresses and maids ... Caravans had now rolled in, unfortunately in the first instance, over Lord Poulett's centuries'-old smooth lawns, for temporary accommodation, and a band of helpers began to picnic round Miss Puttock and Miss Phillips, who by now had the air of Shackleton and Captain Cook.

At Malvern, College was now looking desolate, and wholly unbearable. One of the saddest sights, as I finally drove away, was Stanier, left to guard the wreckage of a school over which he had so long and so proudly exercised loving care ...

At Hinton, railway containers were now pouring their contents into the house, and staff and maids began to play a complicated game of 'Happy Families'; 'Have you the top of a yellow wardrobe with I think grapes on it?' 'No, but I have the bottom of a mahogany, I think chest of drawers!' And the sorting of the tops, middles and tails of 167 black iron bedsteads, not constructed by the same makers!

Under the supervision of Miss Dalby and Miss Williams, the entire contents of Summerside and the Benhams, together with a large amount from the Mount and Ryall, were transported

of that road. Ryall was taken in 1905 to house the sanatorium and provide overflow accommodation, and in 1907 the house next to it, The Mount, was leased: the latter had been kept as a school for some years by Miss Rosa Burley. Described in 1894 as 'an essentially high-class establishment', it had then been in Miss Burley's charge for only a short time. Her own records show that the moods of the visiting violin master caused her concern: he was the still unknown Edward Elgar, forced reluctantly to supplement his meagre income by teaching in several schools and coming to The Mount for one day each week. By 1906 a series of misfortunes caused Miss Burley to close her school; her former landlords began in 1907 to lease out the property to Miss Poulton, Miss Greenslade and the new co-principal, Miss Mitchell.

Miss Poulton and Miss Greenslade lived at The Mount for a period. Intended as a junior house for the smaller girls, it took some time to get underway. Young Kathleen Hector, who had joined as a pupil in 1906, had returned to help out at the school. One of the little girls in the group that established the house was Barbara Wallington who was to become better known as Mrs. Chaning-Pearce. She has long associations with the school as pupil and member of staff; her aunt, Miss Gertrude Chalk, was also a pillar of the school, being in the music department—for some years as its head—for a total of 35 years until 1936. To her must go much of the credit for the strength of the musical life of the school.

12. This picture, taken from Ivydene's garden during a gentle game of croquet, shows the gallery connecting Ivydene Hall and Summerside.

13. Inside, the gallery's rather spartan appearance was softened by careful furnishing.

14.   In 1907 Miss Poulton and Miss Greenslade took over The Mount, where Edward Elgar had taught music to the pupils of Miss Burley. As the Junior House, its 'happy home life' was emphasised, but no exeats or shopping were allowed, lest they 'may be fresh sources of infection'. Parents could visit on Saturday and Sunday afternoons.

In 1909 the school adopted the more impressive name of Malvern College for Girls and was considering the possibility of having a separate senior department for girls over the age of seventeen. By 1910 there was a choice of sixth form courses: either academic work in preparation for public examinations, or a thorough grounding in secretarial subjects, for the typewriter had opened up another career opportunity for women. Still, however, a long uphill struggle lay ahead to persuade society that a career could be as important as marriage for a woman. In 1912 the guest of honour at speech day encouraged the girls to look forward to the possibility of having, 'should such a thing be necessary', to earn their own living in order to fulfill 'that noble ambition of being full of service to their fellows'. But, he went on, 'the highest position a woman could hold was that of wife and mother.' Nevertheless the school had already established a reputation for fitting girls to serve a useful purpose in life, and was seen as a training ground for the offspring of the professional classes rather than as a retreat for the spoilt daughters of the affluent. Although some of its pupils undoubtedly fell into the latter category, at school all girls were required to work hard and purposefully at a curriculum which was unusually broad for girls at that time.

In 1910 the senior girls were provided with separate accommodation when a house called Stoberry—at the top of Clarence Road—was temporarily rented. Eventually, after some change in accommodation, Senior House moved to a newly purchased house in the summer of 1913. This was the original Benhams. The present Benhams, once Christchurch Vicarage, became a middle school house in the 1930s and after much deliberation the old Benhams was demolished in the 1950s. However, a new senior house, Greenslade, has been built on this site in

15.   Old Benhams, the Senior House supervised by Miss Mitchell, was also known as Mitchell Lodge. Ten study bedrooms accommodated students studying for higher examinations, five double rooms were for sisters or friends, while larger rooms had cubicles. The day started with prayers and breakfast at 7.40 a.m., with lights out at 10 p.m.

the 1980s. Miss Mitchell presided over Old Benhams, sometimes known as Mitchell Lodge. After enlargement and modernisation it accommodated 30 of the older girls, some of whom had passed their 21st birthday. Several of them worked in their study bedrooms for public examinations and university entrance—the pioneers of a life-style which was to become so typical of girls at Malvern. Domestic science was also taught, in that most practical of ways: girls cleaned the house themselves and prepared many of their own meals. When the school started to rent in Gilbert Road a semi-detached house called Joyfields as a home for its steward (caretaker) the girls also began to keep poultry in its garden.

This house faced the playing-field which was purchased in 1910 when Sir Henry Foley Grey sold off much of the Foley estate which he had inherited at the turn of the century from his formidable great aunt, Lady Emily Foley. The 13 acres which comprised the 1910 purchase were bought for nearly £2,800, which sounds cheap by today's standards but was not especially so by Edwardian. At the time of the purchase it was used partly as pasture land and

16.   Malvern Cricket Ground in Barnard's Green Road as shown in the catalogue when part of the Foley estate was sold in 1910. The Foley family at this time owned the manor of Malvern.

partly as Malvern Cricket Ground, but might well have had a very different appearance by now if Malvern College for Girls had not bought it: the sale catalogue describes it as 'a highly valuable Building Property as it is level, close to the station, commands very beautiful views and possesses a frontage ... to Barnard's Green Road and ... to Madresfield Road, thus enabling it, when required for building, to be profitably developed by the construction of a road and sub-division'.

The school's reputation for science can be traced back as far as 1911, when the newly appointed Miss Cuthbertson set up the science department. A science laboratory was opened in the grounds between Ivydene Hall and the original Benhams. All girls were encouraged to do both practical and theoretical work, and visiting speakers stimulated interest in natural history and other aspects of science. One of these speakers was Miss Poulton's brother, a

17.   The school's first laboratory was 31ft. by 15ft.

professor of zoology at Oxford University. On another occasion, in 1916, the feasibility of a Channel tunnel from Dover to Calais was discussed—the reality took some 70 years to get started! The first pupil to go to Oxford as a university student was Doris Moss, as early as 1912; she was a scientist, became the school's first graduate in 1915, and went on to teach science in Cardiff. Her contemporary, Minnie Gosden, became a doctor in the British Colonial Service, working in Cyprus, Trinidad, Africa and Fiji.

In 1912 a science society was established as one of several extra-curricular activities. Others included the orchestra which started in 1905, St John's Ambulance and a poetry society founded in 1912. A debating society and Girl Guides were both inaugurated in 1914, while a variety of charitable interests were the well intentioned, if rather patronising, early attempts at community service. In 1914, for example, a £5 donation was made to the United Girls' School Mission in south-east London. It gave advice to mothers on feeding and clothing their children, as well as helping to supply medical needs, including surgical appliances for those too poor, in that pre-National Health Service era, to buy them for themselves. Clubrooms were 'instituted for the factory boys and girls' to keep them off the streets, and the genteel girls of Malvern were encouraged to go to help at the settlement when they left school. Since about 1905 they had also given regular support to the Ivydene cot, the annual subscription reaching a generous £25 by 1914. This was to support a bed at an orphanage in Arnside, near Carnforth; the school received 'news and photos of the dear little children who occupy our special bed while waiting to be adopted by some kind people who have no children of their own'. Sometimes the girls enjoyed hearing 'funny stories of the dear little mites who have never before known what it is to be lovingly cared for ... it shews us a sad side of other children's lives, but it is a great pleasure to be able to help them and to make them happy.' Although this smacks of Lady Bountiful, it was an attempt to arouse a social conscience and the sums donated were large for that time.

In 1912 the school acquired yet another co-principal in Miss Kate Dawson, a mathematics graduate of London University which, since its foundation in the 19th century, had been prepared to treat women in a far more egalitarian way than the male strongholds of Oxford and Cambridge. Able, very well-qualified and charming, she had a profound influence on the school's development over the next 15 years until she and Miss Poulton fell out. She had been Senior Mistress at the St Margaret's Clergy Daughters' School at Bushey; a former head girl of the Bushey school later joined Miss Dawson at Malvern to help with the teaching of mathematics. Their work emphasised the importance of the academic life of the school and

its refusal to go along with the 19th-century view that subjects like mathematics were not suitable for frail female minds. By 1914 women graduates were also teaching classics, history, English, science and geography. Visiting teachers provided a change of face and an extension to the curriculum: girls looked forward to 'Monty's lectures', given by kindly old Louis Montagnon, who came every Tuesday to talk about history and literature. Miss Severn Burrow, of a well-connected local family, received girls at her home in St James' Road to teach them 'life drawing', one of the models being a donkey!

Miss Dawson's interest was not merely in the academic side of school life: she showed particular enthusiasm for lacrosse, which is still so strong at the school and was very popular with the girls. Like the other three principals, she put her own money into the business and in 1913 became responsible for running the Junior House in The Mount. Classes continued to be held at Ivydene Hall, convenient for attendance by girls living in any school property.

In 1913 the Old Girls' Association was founded, its first secretary being Kathleen Hector. An ivy leaf—symbolic of Ivydene, the first home of the school—was adopted as its emblem and

18. Miss Kate Dawson, a Principal from 1912 until 1928. At her last Speech Day she said, 'We have tried to build a lasting tradition of sound work and a high standard of conduct and true Christian fellowship in service to God and our generation'. She died. aged 86, in December 1957, leaving money so that a prize could be given annually for mathematics, the subject which she taught.

19.   The gifts presented to the Principals in 1914 on the occasion of the college's 21st birthday were photographed for posterity. At the back is a list of the subscribers, presumably the names of the girls in the school at the time, embellished round the edge with ivy, symbolising the name of the school's original home in Ivydene.

'Union is Strength' as its motto. The original members numbered 47, rising to the current total of about 3,000, many of whom enjoy the annual reunions. In 1929 it began the tradition of an annual dinner in London in addition to the annual weekend reunion in Malvern itself. In its early years a room or two could be kept available for use by the numerous old girls who came back to spend a weekend in school, but this is no longer practicable.

The period of the outbreak of the First World War was a time for reflection as well as expansion. The school celebrated its coming of age in 1914 and a long established member of staff, Mrs. Hogben, wrote its first history, published in the magazine and invaluable for understanding the early development of the school. Each of the principals received a handsome gift to mark its 21st birthday. Gentle Miss Greenslade was given a silver tea-set; business-like Miss Poulton received a set of the *Dictionary of National Biography*; the elegant Miss Mitchell had a gold watch, while even the relative newcomer, Miss Dawson, received a travelling clock.

On a more serious note, the declaration of war against the Kaiser's Germany created patriotic fervour. War was still seen as a necessary evil with more than a dash of glamour about it: names like the Somme and Passchendaele were unknown, so disillusion had not yet set in. The school donated £4 10s. to the Belgian refugees who had settled in Malvern after the German invasion of their country which occasioned war. The girls happily embarked on knitting and sewing comforts for the troops entrenched in the fields of Europe. Within one period of three weeks they produced 115 long, wide scarves and 120 pairs of mittens, and were delighted with their letters of thanks on behalf of the recipients. It was all rather unreal, until news of casualties—like Miss Poulton's nephew, who was killed in action in 1915—began to change attitudes to war.

Although the 21st birthday was an occasion for some celebratory back-patting and congratulations, it was by no means a matter of resting on laurels already won. More property was taken in and around Avenue Road, while modernisation of houses continued with the installation of electricity and central heating, as had been provided for Ivydene Hall in 1913. The additional property was at first rented but some was later purchased when the owners were willing to sell. It was at that time a common practice even for quite affluent people to rent rather than buy their homes. Leasehold property was much more readily available than it has become today after successive governments have changed the law on renting property—a development which has to a large extent dried up the well of leasehold living accommodation. Though Fairlawn, a large house in Imperial Road opposite Great Malvern railway station was rented for only a brief period, other houses—Lindfield, Abbotsmead, Avenue and Hatley St George—became a more lasting extension of what was beginning to be seen as the Poulton-Greenslade empire.

From 1915 until 1925 Lindfield was used as a second Senior House where girls were trained in domestic science, including 'mothercraft' and carpentry. Presumably, making furniture from old packing cases was part of wartime efforts to prove that the middle classes favoured thrift. For about nine years Lindfield was under the watchful eye of Mrs. Kendle, a trained nurse who had seen service in the Boer War at the turn of the century. Before its occupation by Malvern College for Girls, Lindfield had for many years been a school for young ladies run by the Misses Graham, so here was yet another instance of Miss Poulton and Miss Greenslade proving their own tenacity, outdistancing some of their numerous late 19th-century rivals. A vice-principal was appointed on a salary starting at £150 a year, rising by five annual increments to £200, and she took overall responsibility for Lindfield. This was Miss Pulham, a woman of high ideals, unfortunately known to girls and staff of the late 20th century only through the Pulham Cup, awarded to the house with the highest number of points won for various academic and other achievements. For years, at the end of each term, frantic form staff may have thought rather uncharitably of the name Pulham as they feverishly struggled to equate alphabetical grades with numerical points to arrive at the magic numbers which determined the recipients of the Pulham Cup. Miss Pulham herself left the school in 1928.

20.   Lindfield shortly before its acquisition by Malvern College for Girls.

21.   Facilities for domestic science in the early 1920s would not do today, as this obviously staged photograph reveals. Parkfield, a large house in extensive grounds at the junction of Victoria Road and Albert Road, replaced Lindfield as a school of Domestic Science for students over 17 years of age. Enquiries were made of previous schools as to whether applicants were daughters of gentlefolk 'using that word not necessarily with reference to birth or social position, but to their right upbringing of their daughter and their co-operation with your ideals and school regulations for her'.

Abbotsmead, which has been the school sanatorium since 1966, became the home of the original founders—and of the dreaded Polly Pierrot, Miss Greenslade's pet parrot, whose charms were less evident to others than to its indulgent owner.

Avenue House, bought for £2,200 in 1917, provided yet another house for seniors and had the luxury of a reference library as well as classrooms and study bedrooms. At the same time the teaching of science was expanded, with a chemistry laboratory separated from the biology laboratory by a small coaching room. This growing provision for science teaching made clear a commitment to a balanced education for girls, and was remarkable for its time. It comes as no surprise, therefore, to find that Ella Stratton, who wrote the words of the school song, went to medical school in 1918—one of the first women doctors from a school which has produced many. Another girl, Doreen Wallace, won an exhibition to Somerville College, Oxford, and went on to become a highly successful author. She failed, however, to match the output of another old girl of the school, Barbara Cartland, whose entry in *Who's Who* is the longest in that vast tome, and whose prodigious output set a record of 23 books published in one year alone.

There was fun as well as hard work in those early years, and the opportunity to let off steam on the games fields. Miss Whetham came to teach games in 1917 and was still here 30 years later with her excited, if disconcerting, cry of 'Shoot yourself'. In the summer there were picnics and at other times there were concerts and talks in Malvern. In 1912, for example, the girls went to the Assembly Rooms to hear Ellen Terry talk on Shakespeare's 'triumphant heroines' and, despite a severe cold, 'the clearness of her diction and her wonderful voice management struck us all'. In 1916 and 1917 they went to hear Clara Butt, the renowned contralto.

Hatley St George, a large house in five acres, was rented in 1917 and purchased in 1924. At first under Miss Dawson's humane rule, for nearly half a century it was used as the Junior Department, where so many little girls had their first taste of life at Malvern. Next door, Beaufort was also taken in 1919 for use as part of the preparatory department but eventually became a house to accommodate resident staff.

As a business, Malvern College for Girls was clearly thriving. Four women—Miss Poulton, Miss Greenslade and the later arrivals, Miss Mitchell and Miss Dawson—had ventured their own money into an enterprise which must at times have looked uncertain. Enormous social change occurred in the first two decades of the 20th century, the Great War having a dramatic impact on lives and fortunes. Those four women—each with her own special contribution to make to the success of the school—could not have known that the horrors of the years from 1914 to 1918 would alter the position of women in society in ways undreamt of in the halcyon pre-war era. If we cast ourselves back to the time that they risked so much, their courage and achievement seem the more remarkable. By 1915 their success led them to consider it desirable to appoint an accountant to spare Miss Mitchell who had responsibility

22.   Avenue House was bought in 1917. It housed the reference library and had both classrooms and study bedrooms for girls working for higher examinations.

23.   Hatley St George housed the Junior Department, playing an important part in the school's history from 1917 until 1963. After the school sold the house it was transformed into residential apartments.

for two houses as well as carrying much of the burden of the financial administration. The first school accountant, however, was unlikely to have been left with an entirely free hand—Miss Poulton was too interested in this side of affairs to have relinquished complete control and she was not an easy woman with whom to work. It was rumoured that Miss Mitchell's departure in 1917 resulted from differences of opinion with Miss Poulton, and Miss Dawson's departure in 1928 was certainly due to a personality clash with Miss Poulton.

The school now controlled a large amount of property in the area around the main railway station so it is worth considering the effect that the school's growth had on the town. It employed several teachers, who were often brought in from quite distant places to board in the manner that was customary for the spinsters who at that time formed the backbone of the teaching staff at any girls' school. Some impact was also made on employment of local people, for as each house was taken over, it would require more domestic and ground staff to maintain an establishment for increasing numbers of pupils. Just as the water-cure had opened opportunities for locals to earn a living in the 19th century, so Malvern College for Girls, together with other independent schools, offered a 20th-century equivalent. The relationship between employer and employee was still very unequal, the paternalism of the employer reflecting the class divisions which permeated society. In this light we can understand more fully the enquiry which led to one applicant for the position of maid being told that at the Girls' College 'we do not give beer money ... but cocoa twice a day and tea three times, and a very comfortable home.'

The expansion of the school clearly indicates its growing reputation, so it is now appropriate to consider what it offered parents who sent their daughters here, and how the girls themselves saw school life.

Chapter Three

School Life in the Early 20th Century

Boarding school life has changed considerably over the years, though the basic ingredients do not change. For those in charge, the practical matters of teaching, feeding, accommodating and caring for large numbers of adolescents demand enormous reserves of energy and ingenuity. For the young themselves, loneliness or lack of self-confidence can be a heavy cross to bear when all around seem happy, motivated and successful. For everyone, life in a community requires individual adjustments to be made. Unfortunately, much evidence of life in the early years of Malvern College for Girls has been lost, but it is still possible to build up quite a vivid picture from a variety of sources. Important among these are the reminiscences of Old Girls who have so helpfully responded to pleas for information; the earliest school magazines— at first produced sporadically, and painstakingly handwritten—are also a rich vein to mine; but perhaps one of Malvern's most unusual sources is the exercise book containing details of the matrons' duties in Edwardian times. Its anonymous writer was also, unwittingly, very amusing for the modern reader: learning of the domestic arrangements for their predecessors has had some of today's pupils laughing in disbelief at the level of hygiene considered suit- able for teenage girls in an era in which the word 'teenager' had not been coined and the young subordinated their wishes to those of their 'elders and betters'. Indeed, this phrase is unattractive—if not incomprehensible!—to today's young. But there are also certain aspects of a way of life now gone which have some appeal. The idea of maids helping to carry, sort and pack clothes arouses some envy; being waited on at meal times also generates enthusiasm in today's girls for whom carrying away their own dirty crockery is sometimes too onerous a task.

The matrons' book tells us that hair was to be brushed once a week and washed three times a term (twice if a very short term or if the girls had colds, etc). The laundry allowance provides an interesting commentary on the pre-washing machine age: nightdresses, woollen combinations and bodices were changed once a fortnight, while stockings and knicker linings were changed each week. Teaching staff, all resident, were permitted to send only one blouse a week, dresses being charged extra. Face towels were changed every week 'unless not soiled', while bath towels, changed fortnightly, presented special problems: 'have to go half one week and half another, as there are not enough to go round'. Sheets, too, may have been in short supply: '1 Sheet and Pillowcase to be changed on beds every fortnight. Top Sheet to bottom, and bottom to laundry'. Menstruating girls were coyly described as 'not well' and required to take extra rest, usually lying down after dinner. They were not allowed to play games, do drill or even go for walks for three or four days 'according to their condition' and were supplied with the washable diapers which preceded today's disposable towels and tampons. Today parents are often keen for their daughters to catch German measles in childhood to minimise the risk of having it in later life when pregnant and perhaps harming the unborn child. But at the beginning of the century there was widespread fear of infections, even those which today we regard, with benefit of better medical knowledge and treatment, as quite mild. Perhaps this explains why the arrangements for baths were fairly generous for the time: 'The little ones have three baths a week, and the older girls two, except in summer when they get hot and dusty, then 3 for all if possible'. However, when they went swimming only one hot bath was allowed!

Some of the ideas on catering which were current at the time have also been preserved in the matrons' book: 'In early spring when eggs are cheaper buy in quantities up to 1,000 to be put down in Water Glass (Cook does this). Juniors have them scrambled about once a week either for tea or breakfast.' Such a treat is rather different from the personal recollections of Peggy Edwards who arrived at Junior House, now The Mount, in 1912. 'Doorstep bread and butter for tea' greeted her and she was disconcerted to find that boiled milk was served four times a day—at breakfast, elevenses, tea and supper: 'I only managed to drink it by taking a deep breath and drinking it down quickly without tasting or smelling it'.

On Sundays, tea made with milk was equally unpalatable. Miss Poulton came into dinner and had on the top table girls whom she thought needed feeding up. In 1914 she wrote:

> I am entirely in sympathy with all you say about the necessity of good nourishing food while girls are developing in all sorts of ways: in fact we have the character of holding almost too strong views in that point! We weigh every girl in the school on arrival each term and at the end.

She clearly would have had little sympathy with modern ideas on diet, and Peggy Edwards paints rather a daunting picture of a typical meal:

> The rule was two helpings of first course always and one of pudding. There was always milk pudding which was served with 'spotted baby', 'treacle baby' or other boiled puddings or fruit, except on Sunday when we had white blancmange and stewed fruit.

Miss Poulton was respected by the girls and showed a genuine concern for them, telling them to go and put on a long-sleeved vest if their arms seemed cold. She struggled valiantly with food shortages in the First World War and her good housekeeping was not confined to what went on in the kitchen. Always ready to snap up a bargain, she went to sales to buy furniture. She kept her ear to the ground for any demolition work going on in the neighbourhood so that she could buy up bricks and windows which would match those of college property when her numerous and often ingenious plans for extension came to fruition. Architectural salvage was a field in which Miss Poulton was pioneering long before it became fashionable in the 1980s and 1990s.

When Peggy Edwards was at school, the total number of girls was 99, and no two girls had the same Christian name. If, when a new girl arrived, there was another of the same name, the newcomer would use her second name or choose another. At the end of each term before the First World War a birthday party was held for all the girls who had had a birthday during the term. Everyone attended in their white frocks, with woolly shawls in the winter, to enjoy the special tea at which the names of the birthday girls were read out. This was followed by dancing and games.

Miss Mitchell went to Junior House each Sunday evening to read out marks from the report books, and then read to the little ones while they drank the soup which was a Sunday treat to replace the ubiquitous milk. She also took prayers and bible classes, supplementing the vicar's preparation of confirmation candidates and leaving a lasting impression on many young minds: 'When she left in 1917, we lost more than just a beloved Head of Senior House'.

The Middle School at this period was almost entirely housed in Ivydene Hall, called simply 'the Hall'. Just a few girls slept at Lindfield or Abbotsmead. Peggy Edwards wrote a fascinating account of school life in her time. On Sundays,

After dinner came an hour's letter writing in the classroom and then another walk, round the Horseshoe this time, the Juniors going by St. Anne's Well and the Seniors by Wells Road. It was always our hope, coming from Church on Sunday morning, that we would be passing the entrance to the Priory School [a boys' preparatory school in Dr. Gully's former home—now the offices of Malvern Hills District Council at the junction of Avenue Road and the lower end of Church Street] as the boys got there. They always marched from Church and if we were passing their entrance they had to mark time till we went by. That always gave us great joy and amusement—though I don't think we were much interested in them as boys. After the walk on Sunday afternoon came tea and then an hour's silent reading of library books in our sitting rooms. There were three—the one opposite the dining room was used by the junior forms. The chairs were all hard dining room chairs and there was little comfort. The middle forms used the studio where there was rather more comfort and the fifth and sixth forms sat in the girls' drawing room—known as the G.D.R.—which was on the right as one entered through the front door. Opposite was Miss Poulton's drawing room where occasionally one was sent to practise on the piano, and where Miss Poulton and Miss Greenslade interviewed parents. Next to that was the Principals' study, in the window of which Pierrot the parrot had his cage. In the summer he would be brought into the garden and I, with others, spent time trying—without any success whatever—to teach him to say 'damn'. Many were the green feathers I have had to try to paint, but having no gift at all that way, my efforts were always just daubs. On Sunday evenings we had an hour's hymn singing at which we chose the hymns we liked to sing. After Miss Pulham came she usually took this ... At 7 o'clock we put on our best hats and went to supper wearing them so that, going straight to bed from the dining room we took them upstairs with us. Speech Day was the high spot of the summer term and the Prizes were given, as the

24. The girls' drawing room: piano playing was the forerunner of the television—a pleasant diversion for those who chose to sew or chat, but presumably something of a distraction for others trying to read or write.

25.   Pupils and staff about 1913: a. Junior House; b. Staff.

school got too big for the Hall Gym, in the Assembly Rooms. [these, the nucleus of the present Malvern Winter Gardens complex, were opened in 1885] There was a rehearsal the day before ... Prizes were hard to come by, being given only for Distinction in Public Examinations. There were no form prizes.

When the school was small, part of the playing field was grown for hay and there was a hay party with a picnic tea when it was cut—and of course the school sports came afterwards. There was a horse kept for mowing the courts and called 'Charley' . He was quite partial to a tasty bit of school hat—the old boater variety if he could get near enough to the pavilion and anyone had left one on the palings round it.

In the early days, as was usual in girls' independent schools, there was no uniform except a red and blue striped hatband worn on a black straw boater. Later on, red and blue became the basis of the school uniform colours though the pattern of the clothes changed from time to time. Muriel Langley (1904-7) long remembered how frills at the neck and cuffs of her red serge blouses scratched, and how thankful the little girls were when the serge was changed to cashmere. A little later, in winter, Peggy Edwards wore

the School Dress in navy serge with a velvet collar and box pleats hanging from the shoulders with a red ribbon tie and a red girdle. They were warm, comfortable and quite nice to look at.

In summer it was navy tunics with pink candy stripe blouses as in Middle School but the tiny ones had frilly collars. When Miss Dawson gave us ties to wear with them, instead of the navy satin bows known as 'cats' ears' we had before, it was considered a great privilege. In the winter at the Hall we had red school blouses with detachable linings—the linings were washed frequently, the blouses less so. Tunics were not allowed after dinner at the Hall and skirts had to be worn under them in the morning—with a blazer on top it became a three decker. Brown stockings—which the laundry always reduced to the colour of those worn by the Blue Coat boys within a few weeks—were worn till after games and then black ones so that it was impossible to be lazy and not change when one came in from the field. Tape

26. Every programme for the school's earliest dramatic productions—like every copy of the earliest school magazines—was painstakingly copied out by hand, with a care and devotion unknown to the philistines of the age of the photocopier!

27 & 28.   An extension at the side of Ivydene Hall provided the school's first gymnasium and studio.

29.   Girls were encouraged to take fresh air and exercise. Here a gentle game of tennis is played.

loops were sewn on the top and the stockings were fastened together before being sent to the laundry, which must have saved the matrons several hours of sorting. On Wednesday or Saturday afternoon we darned them! On Sundays in summer we wore white serge costumes.

Town, unless one was 'out' with parents was always out of bounds and every so often the Head Girl of the form took a shopping list and the form mistress did the shopping. She must have had a difficult time because we were very fussy about the shape, colour and everything else of the pens, pencils, rubbers, etc that we asked for ...

1916 saw the Tercentenary of the birth of Shakespeare and Sir Frank Benson's Company played in the Assembly Rooms, the College going to two or three of the plays. There was a lecture too, and later on came the inevitable homework of an account of the celebration to be written. There was a visit to Worcester Cathedral, too, ... We were taken over the Cathedral by the Very Rev. Dr. Moore Ede, the Dean, who showed us King John's tomb and said he was one of the two men we can be certain went straight to hell—unfortunately he did not tell us who the other was! The other highlight of the afternoon was a wonderful tea at the Deanery.

Friday afternoons were mostly taken up with Mr. Montagnon's lectures. During the war he took literature ... one week and talked about the war the alternate weeks.

Guiding started in Form IV in the summer term of 1914 so the Malvern College companies were among the very early ones ...

When Armistice came in 1918 our first act was to assemble in our houses for prayers. I remember so well singing 'Now thank we all our God.' There were no more lessons that day and in the evening there was a fancy dress dance to which I went as an eastern potentate dressed in Indian cotton bedspreads with another made into a turban!

Empire Day was regularly celebrated in schools throughout the country, and Malvern College for Girls showed patriotism by wearing guide and cadet uniform at prayers and morning classes.

Life in a boarding school often fails to provide the privacy which many people, young and old, value. Whether privacy from one's peers or from those in authority, it is only in recent years that the need for it has been properly recognised. In the summer term of 1918 Audrey Fox recalled going up to her room to find that Miss Poulton, whom many girls feared, had been round, thought her drawers untidy and had tipped their contents on to the bed.

One girl vividly recalled an unusual feature of Ivydene—its fire escape, which was simply a rope fastened to a pulley near a fourth-floor window. This was eventually replaced by a proper iron fire escape, but only after the pine partitions, erected to give privacy between beds, were removed because they were deemed a fire risk.

The admissions books for the early 20th century offer some commentary on social life then. Only the affluent could afford to educate their daughters privately, and the declared purpose of one such father's investment conjures up for us a picture of a society—and a world—long forgotten. The girl was to be prepared for life in India by the time she was 18, and her education must equip her 'to rule a large household'. In somewhat different vein, another girl was solemnly entered in the book as 'Overgrown. Heart too small for body. No violent exercise'. Another poor child's 'want of balance' prevented 'graceful movement'—a social disadvantage indeed! Domestic strife was occasionally revealed, too: one child was 'never to be left alone with mother'. The principals admitted that 'we dearly like tinies of six and seven when we can get them, but girls of any age are very welcome'. In a letter written in July 1914 they paid tribute to the kindliness shown by Miss Dawson:

30.   Riding was always popular—escorts were provided for lessons which cost 7s. 6d. in the school's early years.

31.   Hockey must have been rather difficult to play in long skirts such as these.

32.   Guiding was very popular for many years. This picture was taken in 1918.

Miss Dawson, who became resident Principal of the Junior House a year ago, has greatly endeared herself to all the children who confide to her ready ear their little joys or woes, and we hear on all hands how satisfied the parents are and how entirely Miss Dawson has gained their confidence. At the present time we have a perfectly charming set of 22 little girls from 6 to over 14 and they are as happy as children can be and working well under a thoroughly experienced staff of teachers. The same mistresses give lessons in drawing and painting, elocution, piano etc as teach the students at our Senior House for nothing can be too good for laying the foundations of a useful and accomplished woman's life ...

In neither [Junior/Intermediate] of our houses is 'larking' allowed. Silence at night in the bedrooms is our rule for the protection of all: upon these points we feel strongly the need of a quiet time for rest and sleep as both work and play make greater demands upon the girls' vitality than they did in former days.

The school was unusual in giving older girls more liberty than most other schools of the time: provided a girl had 'passed the Rubicon' of her 17th birthday she could graduate to the Senior House which had been instituted at the end of 1909. Sometimes girls stayed as pupils in Senior House until well into their twenties. To the impressionable girls of the middle school they seemed a race apart 'reclining in deck chairs or on rugs'. Their hats were 'a veritable flower garden when they went to the Priory on Sunday'. They lived in those days in the original Benhams, adjacent to Ivydene Hall. One father had made enquiry about sending his daughter who was uncertain about her future. He was told,

33.   Games featured more strongly during and after the First World War. Miss Whetham and Miss Dawson encouraged competitive hockey and lacrosse, as well as netball. This photograph of the Hockey XI shows Miss Whetham in the back row; beloved by generations of girls, she lived to be over a hundred. Seated on the left is another legendary figure, Barbara Wallington (Mrs. Chaning-Pearce).

34.   Drill was probably less popular!

We find it a frequent phase. It was precisely with a view to steadying such wavering that we organised a Senior House as a much needed interlude between the routine of the purely schoolgirl life and the larger liberty of university life of which a girl cannot make the best use until she possesses a greater sense of responsibility.

Some letters to parents reveal a commendable frankness. Of a girl who had been ill it was written in 1914:

> A... tries to get her own way too much and this is bad for the growth of self-control. We have all spoilt her a bit ... I dread her becoming as she grows older one of the hysterical women who, instead of being a help to their relations, are an ever-increasing burden, and I should like A... to be gently led into a more robust way of viewing things.

Although some Old Girls have denied that snobbery existed in the school, unquestionably it did. In September 1914 a note written by one of the principals to a mother hoping to send her daughter to the school clearly states that, having learned that the girl's father 'is in retail business ... we very much regret that we are therefore unable to receive your daughter.' Although claiming to have no personal objections to people in trade, the principals 'at the present critical moment ... dare not run counter to prejudice even when we do not ourselves sympathise with it.' Expediency seems to have triumphed over principle in those anxious days of the war when uncertain finances led to the withdrawal of several pupils. The irony of the school's success depending on the business acumen of the principals never seems to have been voiced. Not yet was anyone so blunt as Miss Judson, principal of the Abbey School in Malvern Wells: in the 1920s she complained about the adverse effect on her school of quarrying stone from the Malvern Hills and carting it in lorries with metal rimmed wheels past the school so that the noise and vibration interfered with teaching. Why, she wanted to know, should certain businesses, like running a school, be jeopardised by another business such as quarrying?

Chapter Four

Purchase of the Imperial Hotel

In the uncertain period at the end of the First World War the indomitable Principals took an ambitious proposal to their chief adviser, Mr. (later Sir) William Joynson Hicks, a Member of Parliament who rose to become Home Secretary. The grandest and most luxurious hotel in the area—the *Imperial*—was on the market; they wanted to buy and adapt it for school use. The *Imperial Hotel* had been built in 1862 at the height of the water-cure era, when Malvern was developing from an obscure village to a spa town. As Sir William later observed at the opening of the former hotel as the school's main building, they evidently 'felt that even in the darkest days of the War, no matter what befell the British Empire, the school must go on'. This rather heavy joke produced laughter and applause from an audience still smarting from the effects of a war which had caused such terrible suffering that it was fondly believed that it must end all war. The purchase of the *Imperial Hotel* was remarkably enterprising even for a woman as determined as Miss Poulton, and at the opening Sir William still seemed taken by surprise at what the genteel lady Principals had achieved when the conventional female role was to cling nervously to the coat-tails of a man.

But change was in the air, and these ladies were not cast in the traditional female mould. They had a long record of successfully investing in the unfashionable and uncertain business of girls' education. The middle classes from whom they drew their clientele still rated the education of their sons much more highly than that of their daughters and, as several letters in the 1914-18 period reveal, some parents found that the war had financially embarrassed them. Fees at Malvern were not cheap and the admitted difficulties for parents in finding the money to pay them did not, on the face of things, augur well for the future.

The Principals, however, had an innate—perhaps prescient—belief in a cause that was to prove significant and indeed vital to the now accepted doctrine of sexual equality: girls, whatever their talents, must be properly educated. As early as 1915 a prospective parent had been bluntly told that this was necessary 'in order that they may be as efficient and self reliant as possible and fitted to follow some career when schooldays are over'. True independence and equality can come only from the ability to earn one's own living without being obliged to find a husband; the prerequisite of this is a sound education and training appropriate to the individual's needs. The Great War had many far-reaching social consequences, which included an unprecedented impact on women's role in society: this had to be re-assessed in the light of their contribution to the war effort, as the government realised in extending the right to vote in parliamentary elections to many women in 1918.

There was another long-term legacy, too: the tragedy of so many young men dying in their prime led not only to grieving families but to a generation of young women destined to stay unmarried. Put in the crudest terms, there were no longer enough men to go round, so thousands of young women perforce sought a career other than marriage. In so doing they showed many married women the road to more interesting life-styles, for it became clear that a good number of 'frustrated spinsters' were actually less frustrated and more fulfilled than

35.   This view from the hills shows, at the left, the *Imperial Hotel* at the turn of the century. Close by rises the spire of Christ Church, built in the 1870s as a memorial to a former vicar of Malvern. Christ Church vicarage became the new Benhams in the 1930s.

36.   Avenue Road was cut through fields to provide access from Great Malvern to the new station. The station, the *Imperial Hotel* and the Avenue Road bridge were designed by E.W. Elmslie as a fitting welcome for the well-to-do who came to Malvern for the water-cure. In the centre of this picture horse-drawn cabs can be seen, waiting to meet the frequent trains and transport passengers to the town's many hotels and boarding houses.

37.   The *Imperial Hotel* from the south.

38.   The Broad Walk, now known as the terrace, to the west of the *Imperial Hotel.*

their married sisters bowed down by the demands of dominant or patronising husbands and domestic chores. Ample evidence of the new woman was to be found at the retitled Malvern Girls' College where a growing body of mostly unmarried professional women trained their pupils not simply to become compliant and competent wives and mothers, but also to hold down responsible jobs in a world less obsessively geared to the values and demands of men. Not least of the attractions was the opportunity to earn a decent salary and retain control of the spending of it.

But what of the building itself, so bravely taken on by these extraordinary women in 1919? In mid-Victorian times it had been opened as part of a scheme to impress wealthy visitors coming to Malvern for the water-cure first introduced in the 1840s by Dr. Wilson and Dr. Gully. The railway network had rapidly extended across the country from the 1840s onwards, and in the 1850s there was much talk of extending further west, from Worcester to Hereford. E. W. Elmslie, a London architect, produced particularly interesting plans for a station, bridge and hotel at Great Malvern, as well as a rather more modest station and hotel at Malvern Link. The Great Malvern scheme was his grandest achievement, reflected in the fact that it still stands in its entirety, whilst the *Malvern Link* hotel was demolished some twenty years ago—to the shame of those who permitted it to happen. The station at Malvern Link has also been much altered, but the masterpiece at Great Malvern is now a listed building which cannot be altered or demolished. Although sadly damaged by a serious fire in 1986, it has been restored to its former glory, though the 'worm', a tunnel which provided direct underground access to the *Imperial Hotel*, has not been in use for many years. Splendid though the station is, its design ensured that it should be almost out of sight from the hotel—just as the railway track itself was hidden in a cutting for much of its length.

Soon after the *Imperial Hotel* was opened a guide book was published with details of the building and the facilities it offered. It is well worth quoting from this at some length for it provides an insight into the hotel—and the 19th-century style—which is unobtainable from any other source.

> A truly magnificent building, not unworthy of the unrivalled scenery amid which it stands, ... it was opened to the public on the 11th of August 1862 ... It is substantially built in the Continental Gothic style, in red brick, with Bath and Forest stone dressings, and is conveniently arranged, resembling in general configuration the letter L, so that being six stories high and surmounted by a commanding tower, and situate in the midst of private grounds, extending over three acres of land, it has a very imposing appearance, its peculiarly slated roof and singularly regular outline contrasting well with the general character of the town ...The gate piers, which are very massive, are surmounted with lamps of elegant design, the carved griffins showing to great advantage below them, the gates themselves being of wrought iron, richly foliated. As it will be interesting, no doubt, to examine this noble erection 'from garret to basement', we propose to begin by observing that, in the lowest depths of all, or the sub-basement, there are endless ranges of cellars, out of which, in the sultry summer days, dainty delicacies are delved, which have been cooling there for extended periods of time. Ample room is also given to efficient heating apparatus, the results of which, in winter, are as gratifying as are the Epicurean delights afforded by the other chambers on this level during the sweltering months of summer.
>
> The Basement Floor contains a noble kitchen ... Of course, all the pantries ... and utensils incidental to gastronomical catering of the highest class, are freely provided ...
>
> The principal point of access to the Hotel is through the large Entrance Hall on the ground floor, which has a very fine ribbed ceiling. Two spacious corridors run off from this hall, the one to the north, the other to the east, and both are paved with Maw's tiles, arranged in patterns which have a very bold and pleasing effect. At the end of the northern corridor is a remarkably ample and well-arranged Coffee Room, whose noble proportions, commodious

39 & 40.   The front of the school's main building with the original wrought-iron railings, gates and lamps—all sacrificed in the 1940s as part of the war effort. Sadly, subsequent revelations suggest that the nation's loss of a large fraction of its beautiful Victorian iron-work was quite unnecessary. All the rooms to the left of the main door were doubled in size in 1928, and the picture therefore shows only one set of windows.

arrangements, and tasteful furnishing, constitute it one of the best rooms of the kind in England. It measures 64 ft. in length by 30 ft. in breadth, and in height it is 27 ft.; the ceiling is ribbed and panelled and, by means of enriched beams, divided into three bays. Elegant marble shafts, with elaborately carved capitals and bases, give the necessary support, and the shafts and caps to the windows are treated in the same way.

The Ladies' Coffee Room, which is fitted up with everything which can minister to the comfort and convenience of that section of the Hotel's patrons to whom it is specially devoted, is also on the ground floor. So are also the Table d'Hote, the Board Room, the Manager's and Still Room, as are also the Hotel Offices; and besides these, on the same level, are suites of sitting, bed and dressing rooms, all of which are really beautiful apartments, well finished and luxuriantly furnished throughout.

The Reading Room, which is approached from ... the Coffee Room, is light, airy and cheerful; it is lavishly supplied with English, American and Continental reviews, periodicals, newspapers and books; and every means is taken to have the metropolitan evening papers placed on the tables at the very earliest possible moment.

On the First Floor, and over the Reading Room, are the Smoking and Billiard Rooms ... On the same landing are six suites of bed, dressing and sitting rooms, each suite having its

41.   The grandest room in the hotel was the dining room, also referred to as the coffee room. It is now barely recognisable, with classroom W and the bookshop occupying its heart.

42.   The hotel conservatory became Room A on the ground floor. New rooms, including S, were built over it.

43 & 44.   The hotel lounge became the college dining room, extended in 1928. It is now the senior common room.

own independent offices and adjuncts; and several other apartments, which we cannot describe within our meagre limits, are also located on this level. On the Second Floor are 31 bedrooms,averaging ... 16 ft in breadth; ... There are 30 bedrooms, corresponding in size and general arrangement with those already alluded to, on the Third Floor. The top, or Servants' Floor, contains 28 bedrooms. In all, there are upwards of 100 bedrooms, which are, without exception, lofty and well-ventilated. The carpets, in every part of the building, are of the best description and display good taste in their selection. The furniture, too, is elegant.

The hotel is abundantly supplied with water from a private spring in the tunnel of the Great Western Railway at Malvern Wells, whence it is conveyed by the company's mains direct to the Hotel premises. This is the celebrated Malvern Hill water, so highly commended by the medical men and chemists who have reported upon it. Ample as is this never-failing supply, the Proprietors have wisely taken the precaution to have the water laid on from the town mains too, which, being brought by a very rapid descent from a much higher level, gives a pressure which would be invaluable in the case of a fire—a contingency which has, however, been jealously guarded against in every way.

In fact, the most serious fire that Malvern town had ever suffered took place at the *Imperial Hotel* in June 1896. A man working in the gardens saw, at about 11.40 a.m., flames coming from the roof close to the kitchen and laundry flues. Malvern fire brigade arrived with as much speed as it could manage, but the horses drawing the fire engine were frightened by its defective brakes and bolted past the hotel down to Barnard's Green. A large crowd gathered and helped to remove property from the endangered building and, when a fire engine arrived the pressure of water from the town main was insufficient so the private water source, through the railway tunnel, proved vital. At 1.15 p.m. the Malvern Wells fire brigade arrived to help, but the roof of the west wing collapsed and set fire to the top floor of the building. The tower apparently saved the front wing of the building by preventing the fire spreading along that roof, too. At 1.40 p.m. more help reached the scene in the shape of the Worcester fire brigade, remarkably pleased with itself at making the journey from Worcester in 43 minutes. Its more powerful steam engine achieved more than the smaller engines, now supported also by the Upton brigade. The fire was under control by 4 p.m. but water continued to be played upon it until 7 p.m. and the men then watched carefully throughout the night. The third and fourth floors had been gutted, and even the first and second suffered considerable damage from the water. The hotel was almost fully booked, in anticipation of activities at Malvern College the following week, so it was particularly fortunate that nobody suffered injury, especially since the removal of property from the hotel during the fire had been a somewhat risky undertaking.

The 19th-century guide book gives more detail about the tower, mentioned above as preventing the further spread of the fire.

On the south front, and immediately over the principal entrance, is a large oriel window, three stories high, fitted with elegant tracery, which forms the terminal of the corridors. On the same front is a Tower, 146 ft. high, containing the Grand Staircase, which, like three other flights of stairs, leads from the basement to all the other floors. But it also leads to the top of this tower, where, at an altitude of 100 ft., is an apartment, which serves the purpose of a Belvedere and summer smoking room, from which a most magnificent panoramic view of the country ... is to be had upon any ordinarily fine day.

The spire which originally surmounted this tower was removed some time before the Second World War and the top of the tower itself was removed in 1952. It had become unsafe and a haven for bats which flew into the dormitories and terrified some of the girls.

The roofs are covered with green and purple slates, laid in regular bands, and the ridges, formed of the same, have an ornamental iron cresting.

... Baths, plentifully supplied with the purest Malvern water, are in course of erection, on the most approved Hydropathic principles, so that visitors, staying at the Hotel, will have every advantage afforded by the most celebrated establishments of Hydropathic physicians, combined with the comforts of a first-class Hotel. The extensive grounds, and beautiful gardens and lawns, attached to the Hotel, are being re-arranged so as to afford visitors the privilege of level paths and walks all round the estate which surrounds the building. These will not only take in noble views of the Hills, but remove the complaint, not unfrequently heard, that, at Malvern, there is no place where persons can enjoy a bracing and enjoyable promenade without the labour and fatigue of ascending steep heights—which, in the case of invalids and persons in delicate health, is a great desideratum ...

The new Stables belonging to the Company are now open, and comprise first-class accommodation for horses and carriages. Carriages, saddle-horses, and flys may be had at the Hotel.

These stables were at the bottom of what is now Thorngrove Road, and have for years been used for the servicing of a more modern mode of transport—motor-cars. Among the general comments on hotel arrangements is included a terse 'Smoking not permitted, except in the Smoking Room' and a notice that,

In lieu of all Fees and Gratuities to Servants, a charge of One Shilling and Sixpence per day will be made to each Visitor for attendance. Visitors not having Apartments at the Hotel will

45. A rare view from the quadrangle showing the old hotel conservatory. The foundations were strengthened and rooms were inserted to make full use of the space in this corner of the building.

be charged Sixpence attendance for each meal. The charge for attendance includes the removal of luggage to and from the Hotel, and for all services rendered throughout the establishment.

A proposal in the 1870s for a skating rink on what is now the quadrangle seems to have come to nothing—though it would doubtless have been a popular facility when the hotel was bought for the girls' college.

By the end of the 19th century the water-cure was in decline, not helped by typhoid occurring at Priessnitz House, now Park View, which Dr. Wilson had purpose-built in 1845 as a hydropathic establishment. The *Imperial Hotel* had enjoyed success, but obviously suffered in the decline which affected so many of the hotels and boarding-houses founded on the crest of the water-cure wave. In 1891 it had sufficient space to be able to offer Wellington College accommodation during an epidemic at that boys' public school.

Mr. Moerschell, the proprietor of the *Imperial*, was of German extraction and, although he changed his name to Marshall, oral tradition has it that he was first tarred and feathered and then interned during the First World War, when anyone with even the most tenuous German connection was regarded with suspicion. By this time, rich visitors no longer flocked to Malvern, which was in danger of being destroyed by the stone-quarrying on the hills. This unfortunate combination of circumstances led Frederick Marshall to sell his hotel. Although there was some vague muttering in Malvern about the school's acquisition of the town's grandest building, it is unlikely that many people were interested in so large a structure except the women who already had control of so much property in the immediate vicinity. The purchase price of £32,500 included quantities of furniture and fittings: since the original cost of the building was reputed to be over £80,000 it was, in a sense, a phenomenal bargain, especially since architects estimated that the cost of erecting it in 1919 would have been £250,000. But it was also a building requiring considerable alteration, maintenance and a bank loan which was to be a mill-stone for years to come. One Old Girl, however, referred to a modest saving for parents—they no longer had to supply their daughters with sheets!

Notwithstanding the fact that the hotel advertisements had always claimed that the sanitary arrangements were perfect, the whole drainage system was renewed. Central heating and electric lighting were installed, though it is still possible for the observant to detect the evidence of old gas lighting protruding above the old, blocked-up fireplaces. Rooms adapted

46.   View from the hotel across to the baths. The college adapted the baths complex for science and art teaching. An extra floor was added in the late 1920s.

47.   The school chapel: Miss Dawson was very fond of it and called it the oratory.

for their new purposes set the pattern for generations to come: the rooms on the second floor became the main teaching rooms, the top floor was divided between the music and secretarial departments, while the rest of the building became residential accommodation for the seniors. The swimming bath also needed improvement. The old brine baths were cleared away—as Sir William Joynson Hicks put it at the opening ceremony, it was 'felt that the young ladies at the school would not have rheumatics at their age'. A gallery was inserted in the bath area, and the rest of the building was transformed into a studio and science laboratories. A surprisingly modern curriculum was envisaged: below the science laboratories it was planned to hold 'handyman classes' in carpentry, book-binding and other skills. A gymnasium was provided at Avenue House. When the Bishop of Coventry came in November 1919 to dedicate the former hotel to new service as a school, care was taken to bless the small chapel on the first floor; plans were laid to raise money for a chapel building large enough to hold the entire school but this was one of the few schemes which Miss Poulton failed to realise. Some people think this was just as well: a private chapel tends to isolate a school from the local community but Malvern Girls' College, which has never had a chapel large enough to hold the whole school, developed strong links with Great Malvern Priory.

With the purchase of the hotel the college had proclaimed that it was no longer one of Malvern's numerous little schools, and it had indeed become one of the most important in England, comparable with the great pioneering girls' schools, such as Cheltenham Ladies' College, founded in the middle of the 19th century. As its value, size and importance grew, so did the need for effective management, for the death of its founders—now elderly women—must not mean the end of the school. Sir William Joynson Hicks pointed out at the opening ceremony that although it was a private school, with over three hundred pupils it now had a public responsibility. In the spirit of the age, he went on to proclaim that: 'the building would for many years to come fulfil a far higher purpose in Malvern and the district than it did as a hotel, for the work that it was now undertaking was for the good of the country and for God.' These rather pompous words earned applause.

So, with the acquisition of the new building, the management of the school also changed. As directors, Miss Poulton, Miss Greenslade and Miss Dawson held all the shares and the school became a Limited Liability Company with an advisory Council, which was to become the school's governing body. The original founders, Miss Poulton and Miss Greenslade, devoted themselves exclusively to the increasing administration, while Miss Dawson, better academically qualified than either of them, became the Principal of the College at a salary of £500 a year— a handsome sum for a woman to earn at that time—and also invested £3,500 of her own money in the venture. Miss Poulton and Miss Greenslade drew no salary: each had invested £5,000 of her own money in the school and they were happy to reside together at Abbotsmead with upkeep being paid as part of the working expenses of the college. Miss Poulton had general oversight of the buildings, furniture and grounds, and was very effective at this: numerous repairs and extensions were initiated by her, and her astute purchase of bricks, panelling and various other embellishments from grand houses, coupled with her generosity to the school, meant that in the next 15-20 years it benefited enormously in both financial and aesthetic terms. Miss Greenslade was usually thought of as the gentler of the two founders, and super-vised financial matters. That gentle appearance may well have hidden a strong-minded woman with an incisive mind: she was, after all, a teacher trained at a time when such training was not easily acquired by anyone in her position.

It is perhaps surprising that these independent women had decided to have a consultative council to help direct policy in the future, particularly since the Council had the right to publicise its views to parents if they differed from those of the directors. The Council also had access to buildings, received an annual school report and was to be consulted if any of the principals were changed—the first such occasion occurring in the late 1920s. The original Council consisted of themselves, Sir William Joynson Hicks, the Bishop of Coventry and two very influential local personalities: C. W. Dyson Perrins, a great benefactor of Malvern, and Miss Alice Baird, principal of St James' School, West Malvern—an establishment that might have been seen as a rival to Malvern Girls' College. More likely, such institutions were so rare that those who directed them were glad enough to share problems and solutions.

Chapter Five

Consolidation and Expansion

The 1920s were a period of both academic and financial consolidation. By 1922 the total assets of the school had reached a very healthy £79,970, with the former *Imperial Hotel* itself valued at a conservative £30,812—a figure lower than the purchase price because miscellaneous bits and pieces had been sold, as had the stables and taproom which had been bought with the hotel, but were of no particular use to the school. The courageous purchase of the hotel seems to have produced publicity that led to instant success: within a year over a hundred pupils were added to the total roll. The school's property now included the main building (the former hotel), Ivydene Hall (valued at £5,000), Summerside, Abbotsmead, Avenue and the old Benhams building, on which site Greenslade House now stands. It also owned several acres of playing field and, as we have seen, rented several houses.

On Speech Day 1921 Miss Dawson reported the achievements of the past year. Three houses had been acquired: Standish Lodge, conveniently situated opposite the main building, is still used as accommodation for domestic staff, but Orchard Lodge and Grattanhurst, which housed both girls and staff in Orchard Road, have been disposed of, the latter becoming a bowling green close to Priory Park. The business and administration of the college had grown considerably, so it is not surprising to note that, although Miss Greenslade had been appointed to supervise financial affairs, a College Bursar was now also employed to take charge of the accounts.

48.   The entrance hall is still recognisable—just! At the right is the original door to the headmistress's study and flat; next to that is the door to the conservatory. Elegant furniture stood on a Victorian tiled floor. This has now been replaced by wooden parquet flooring—presumably better at withstanding the impact of all those trunks at the beginning and end of term. The modern visitor may, however, sit quite comfortably in what was once the discreetly windowed office, used at first by the hotel management and later by the bursar.

Miss Dawson's 1921 report was not simply concerned with bricks and mortar, but her account of extensive structural alterations reflects the facilities the school was offering. 'Beautiful rooms' were adapted for the Secretarial School in the south wing of the basement, while almost all the rooms on the top floor were used as music rooms, sound-proof bricks having been used to sub-divide several of the larger rooms. She noted an increase in the number of girls wishing to take up careers involving higher or specialist training: dents were appearing in the traditional mould of young ladies. Alix Kilroy, for example, won an exhibition for history at Oxford at this time: she went on to reach the top of the civil service and become Dame Alix Meynell. Other girls specialised in economics, music and medicine. In 1921 the school had 434 pupils, over 40 of them coming from overseas, binding the school, as the headmistress put it, 'closer to other parts of the Empire'. There were girls whose homes were in Rhodesia, India, Ceylon, Burma, Jamaica, Barbados and Mexico, as well as Sweden, Norway and Russia. Miss Dawson had always attached great importance to allowing older girls greater freedom than that possible for younger ones: it was particularly pleasing to her that the purchase of the *Imperial Hotel* enabled them to live in this building, clearly marking their graduation from the middle school houses occupied by girls up to the age of about sixteen.

As Miss Dawson explained in 1924, the school welcomed both academic girls, preparing them for university, and the less academic who, from the age of 15, followed a different curriculum, aimed at developing any individual talent. This meant that the school had flourishing music, art, secretarial and domestic science departments. The school was proud of the thorough secretarial training it provided; former pupils have expressed their appreciation of it and the school used its trainee secretaries to help with its growing paperwork. It seems, therefore, to have been a mutually satisfying arrangement. As for the music, both individual performers and the school orchestra were very successful: external examiners complimented the school on the standards achieved, and girls worked towards L.R.A.M. diplomas. Domestic science still flourished at Lindfield until 1925 when Parkfield, in Graham Road, was purchased.

In 1922 a gallery was erected in the assembly hall to cope with the ever growing number of pupils. In 1925 Miss Poulton conceived a plan for a new

49.   The ground-floor corridor is now largely denuded of its furniture. Patterned wallpaper and panelling have been replaced by more practical surfaces which can easily be painted and washed.

50.   A detail of the stonework in the tower is very similar to that of the Avenue Road Bridge, designed by the same architect.

51.   The trees in Avenue Road were in their prime in the 1920s—in the 1990s many are reaching the end of their lives. This view shows Malvern at its best against the backcloth of the hills.

52.   A reminder of things we have loved and lost—wrought-iron railings and plenty of parking space!

53. Subsequent building has greatly altered this 1920s view across to the playing fields bought in 1910.

library on school corridor, creating one large sunny room out of two rooms and part of the corridor—probably the area is now used as the geography and computer rooms. The physical education department was delighted with the acquisition of a new hockey and three lacrosse pitches, made possible by the purchase of several acres of Pickersleigh Fields. Riding continued to be available: since 1919 girls had gone to the new Avenue Riding School in Barnard's Green. Owned by E. H. Humphries, it was taken over in the 1960s by Miss Joyce Jeacock who moved it to Merebrook Camp but continued to teach girls from the college. A new dimension was added to the curriculum in 1925 by Miss Greenslade's purchase of the 11-hole golf course on the Wells Common, together with the former Golf House, but this property was eventually sold.

Much had been achieved since those modest beginnings in the front room in College Road. But much still had to be done. Miss Poulton seems never to have been happy unless stretching to the utmost herself, her finances and all who worked with her. She initiated the

54a & b. The assembly hall, once the grand dining room of the *Imperial Hotel*.

THE LIBRARY.

55.   Old Girls have given conflicting information as to where the library was: this looks like the present room D, now the heart of the computer centre.

unobtrusive extension made to the front of the main building in 1927-28, adding new windows and brickwork so perfectly matched to the original that, from the outside, the new is scarcely distinguishable from the old. This extension doubled the size of some rooms, and is most easily detectable in what are now the Senior Common Room and the Geography Room. At the same time 'loggias' were built over the assembly hall that had once been the hotel ballroom. This explains the extension to Classroom F which has offered temptation to generations of girls keen to leave the classroom and go out on the balcony, especially during heatwaves or snow storms. Further extensions were to be made—but they had to wait until a more immediate crisis had been resolved.

     Kate Dawson left in 1928. It is far from clear why she went and records, many of which seem to have been destroyed at this time, give us clues rather than hard facts. The circumstances of her departure were certainly not happy, and it seems that by the autumn of 1927 the Council became aware that Miss Dawson could no longer work harmoniously with Miss Poulton. Plans for her to retire by 1931 were speeded up to secure her departure in the summer of 1928. Quite apart from the evidently difficult negotiations which preceded her departure, it left the school with a financial problem: with Miss Dawson went her own substantial capital investment and a large sum to compensate her for premature loss of her position. In all, the financial cost to the school was £23,000; those who had grown to love and value her undoubted gifts as an able and dedicated teacher saw the loss as incalculably greater even than that. In 1930 she opened a school of her own in Esher and was joined by another long-serving member of Malvern Girls' College staff—Miss South, who had been at the Junior House for 13 years.

56a & b. Two views of school corridor, used since 1919 as the principal classroom area. At the time of these photographs girls would have moved in silence from room to room between lessons.

57. A classroom—but which? Is it J?

58a & b.   The school dining room, now the Senior Common Room, was just inside the front door. It was doubled in size in 1928.

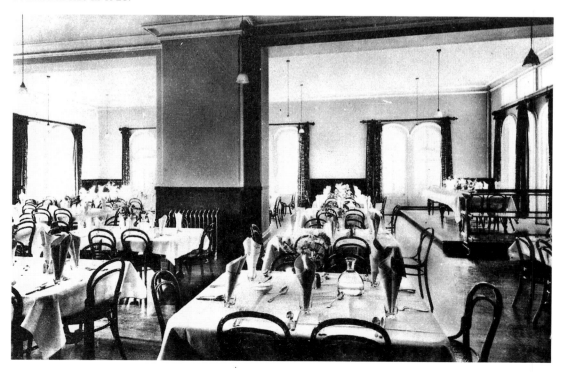

By 1927 Miss Lilian Faithfull had joined the school's Council, and it may well be that her presence had important implications at this time. She had been Principal of Cheltenham Ladies' College, and no doubt blew into Council meetings a strong breath of the fresh air of academic training of a more structured—and possibly of a more ruthless—variety than had hitherto been tried at Malvern. Whatever the details of the power struggle that seems to have gone on from 1927 to 1928, the results included the winding up of the company established in 1919, the setting up of a new company—Malvern Girls' College (1928) Ltd.—and the appointment of a some-what avant-garde headmistress, the redoubtable Miss Iris M. Brooks. She was to hold office for the next 26 years of the school's history, playing a crucial role in establishing its high academic reputation. Perhaps it was significant that she was born in 1893, the same year that the school was founded. She herself claimed at Speech Day 1946 that the day of her birth, 9 August, was the exact date of the school's original foundation in College Road and that the usually accepted date of sometime in September was inaccurate. She was also to celebrate her silver jubilee as headmistress in 1953, the year of the school's diamond jubilee.

On 24 February 1928 the Council decided to place in appropriate papers an advertisement for a headmistress, and on 3 April—less than six weeks later—they had unanimously selected Miss Brooks from a shortlist of five candidates. There is an interesting sidelight to be thrown on the subject of salaries here, indicating the relative scale of priorities of the time. The post of Headmistress was advertised at £700 a year, rising annually by £50 to a maximum of £1,000 plus board, lodging and laundry. At the same time, a graduate teacher earned about £200, while most non-graduates earned a good deal less. Teachers were paid termly, at the end of the term—a system that, for some, was a considerable hardship. In comparison, we may note that in February 1928 the Council agreed to pay a local doctor £2 5s. a year (dissatisfaction having been expressed at a mere £1 11s. 6d.) for every boarder in the school, giving him an income for this part-time work of well over £600 a year! Council members themselves were to receive £5 5s. (well over a week's income for a teacher) for every attendance at a Council meeting! Clearly some felt uneasy at this curious set of priorities, for as early as May 1929 Miss Brooks quite easily secured five per cent increases in the salaries of the longer serving teaching staff, and the Council reduced their own attendance allowances to £2 2s. plus the democratic third class railway fare. This allowance remained unaltered until it was abolished in 1966, when several aspects of school finance were overhauled: the doctor's fee was to be £2 2s. per pupil—a very substantial reduction in real terms—and teachers were to be paid monthly, by credit transfer. These Council resolutions of the 1960s very clearly reflected changing social attitudes.

In 1928 Miss Brooks was provided with a freshly decorated flat, at the front of the main building: to this day, that flat has remained the headmistress's term-time home. Grace Phillips, her friend, came with Miss Brooks to act as her private secretary until 1940. She actually stayed at the school for even longer than Miss Brooks. From 1928 until 1948 she was respon-sible for the lavish ballets performed by the girls, whilst in 1929 she also introduced cricket, which never achieved the popularity of lacrosse. She particularly endeared herself to the girls of Summerside, where she was housemistress from 1940 until 1960. Her former charges still refer affectionately to her as 'Pippy', remembering her concern for them as individuals and her insistence on high standards of courtesy and deportment: generations of Summerside girls knew the correct way to consume their soup!

The Council wanted the popular Miss Pulham to become deputy headmistress with general supervision of the houses and the organisation of the Old Girls. But she declined, leaving at Christmas 1928 to become headmistress of St Peter's School, Folkestone. Miss Dora Puttock, senior mathematics teacher, took over instead, serving from 1929 until 1957 with the

59 & 60.   Science and art teaching has been based next to the swimming pool since the college bought the hotel.

61.   Forbidden territory now, except to Poulton girls for whom it is part of their term-time home.

62.   This students' sitting room is probably now one of the Modern Languages teaching rooms—Q?

rather unfortunate title of Vice-Mistress. In 1969 news of her death reminded many of her associates of her grace, wisdom, humour and integrity.

The late 1920s saw a thorough tightening up of organisation and Miss Young, college bursar since 1923, was relegated to assistant bursar in March 1929 when Mr. J. M. Wright was given the post of bursar. He had responsibility not only for the accounts but also for all college property and for supervision of male staff. At that time all of these were non-academic: men were not yet allowed into the school as teachers, possibly because academic staff were resident. Resident male staff in a girls' school would have raised eyebrows and caused parents to look for another school.

It was decided in March 1929 to go ahead with further extensions which emphasised the school's academic ambitions. Well-equipped new science laboratories and four new 'model' classrooms were provided. The work necessitated adding a floor to the laboratory block, a covered way to the swimming pool, science and art rooms having already been built in 1923. Miss Poulton's comment to the new headmistress was certainly apt: 'I hope the sound of building does not worry you—we are always building here.'

By the autumn of 1929 Miss Greenslade retired from active participation in Council work but, with Miss Poulton, was always ready to put her hand in her purse to further the cause of ensuring that Malvern Girls' College stayed in the van of girls' education. The next grand scheme was getting nearer to realisation and work began on an extensive new wing in 1931, the foundation stone being laid by the Right Rev. Arthur Perowne, Bishop of Worcester, on 3 June 1932. Various members of the school community added symbolic items on this occasion: corn was scattered, symbolising growth and plenty; oil was poured as a symbol of peace and unanimity; salt for truth and friendship and wine for joy and cheerfulness.

63.   The chapel in the 1980s.

The original plans for the new wing included a basement (now Middle School cloak-rooms), a ground-floor assembly hall (York Hall), library and, on top of that, a chapel, for which a fund had been launched by the Old Girls' Association several years before. Since there was a strong feeling that the school should have a chapel built on its own separate site, the plans for a chapel in the new wing were never carried out. In fact, the separate chapel has never been built, though by 1950 over £4,500 had been contributed for that purpose. In 1959 the money was spent instead on modifying the small chapel on the first floor so as to provide a more inviting haven in the main building itself. Pews replaced the old chairs, a parquet floor was laid and an impressive alabaster reredos, depicting the Annunciation, was carved by the young David Wynne. The altar was moved to the wall facing the entrance door, regarded as a somewhat daring change as it was on the north side of the chapel instead of the traditional east. It had the advantage of enabling worshippers to glance westwards through the window to the Malvern Hills in the spirit of Psalm 121, which has for generations been associated with the school: 'I will lift up mine eyes unto the hills from whence cometh my help.' A ballot decided that the residue of the Chapel Fund was to be used to help educate members' children whose fathers had been killed or disabled during the Second World War.

In the 1920s and 1930s when plans for the new wing were being considered, Miss Poulton's nose for truffling out suitable bargains led to some interesting acquisitions, though unfortunately it is not possible to verify all the sources. The State Room from Bohum Court provided panelling for what is now Room Z—the oak room once used for meetings of the school's governing council. The Tudor and oriel windows in the library came from the same source. Tradition claims that the panelling in the library, like the wooden balusters outside it, came from the Hornyold family's mansion at Blackmore Park in the neighbouring parish of Hanley Castle. This seems very likely, since certainly the Blackmore porch graces the external entrance to the new wing, and in the stone work at the top of the porch outside the York Hall the initial letter of 'Hornyold' can still be clearly seen.

It is perhaps as well that the new building got underway in 1931 for it may never have been started had it been left until later. By November 1932 the finance committee expressed serious concern for the school's financial position: it deluded itself into thinking that the drop in the number of boarders suffered by Malvern and other schools was a temporary phenomenon due to the declining birth rate during the First World War. In fact the causes for declining numbers entering private education were much more complex. First, the declining birthrate was not a result of the war—it was a permanent trend resulting from wider knowledge of contraception. Secondly, the worldwide economic troubles of the 1930s put three million people in Britain out of work, and included among the victims the middle class parents who have always formed the backbone of private education. Indeed, economic problems found some other victims very close to home: by 1933 all college staff were required to accept salary cuts. The groundsmen's wages were reduced by five per cent, with the proviso that no-one was to be reduced to less than £2 a week; and teaching staff lost seven and a half per cent of their net salaries. Nationwide, the policy of imposing such reductions hit most government employees, such as teachers, servicemen and civil servants.

In the grip of the financial crisis, Miss Poulton and Miss Greenslade each most generously gave £15,000 of debentures to the college, thus more than justifying the official name of Founders' Library for the magnificent creation above the York Hall. But the school still had debts to the tune of £45,000 and an expected deficit in 1933-34 of £6,000: the cost of running the school in 1932-33 had been £63,400; in 1933-34 it was estimated that 340 boarders and 60 day girls would bring in only £57,400 in fees, and it was impossible to reduce many of the

64. Construction of the new wing. A 16-year-old pupil described the scene in 1932: 'At night-time the massive iron bars looked like the remains of a burned house, against the pale moon and angry sky. At one time the men worked in the darkness of the early evening, and lit huge glowing fires so that they might see more clearly ... Most people wish they could roam about the eerie passages at night-time and climb up on to the second floor ... It is amazing to think that some day, quite soon, there will be furnished rooms there, and that none of the great girders will be in view.' Today, if you know where to look it is possible to detect the join in the outside brickwork; inside the building it is more difficult to pinpoint where the old building ended and the new wing began.

bills that the school faced by any means other than unpopular and undesirable measures such as wage reductions. In May 1933 the financial position was so serious that it looked impossible to complete the new wing.

In November 1932 the Council had, however, acquired a new member, who almost immediately became its chairman; he was Sir Anderson Montague Barlow. By the middle of 1933 he had done what most had thought was the impossible: he had secured a bank loan of £45,000. This task had seemed impossible for two reasons: the first was the worldwide financial crisis, and the second was the reluctance of any bank or insurance company to take as security for a loan so undesirable a property as a collection of school buildings in a provincial town in which hardly anybody was interested. Sir Montague Barlow's magic wand had secured not only the loan, but also his own dominant place on the Council for as long as he cared to stay. He eventually resigned from the chairmanship in 1945, at the age of seventy-seven.

In November 1933 the new building was going according to plan, and the Council noted with pride that 'a Royal lady had hopes that she would be able to perform the ceremony' of officially opening it on 31 May 1934. The 'Royal lady' also permitted the new assembly hall to be named after herself, as Duchess of York. Soon, unexpectedly, to become Queen Consort and then, in 1952, the Queen Mother, she retained a special place in the affections of the

65.   There was great excitement on 31 May 1934, when the Duchess of York opened the new wing. Having declared the York Hall open, she was presented with the key to the Founders' Library by Mr. E. C. Bewlay, the architect. To her left stand Miss Poulton and Miss Brooks.

66.   The York Hall.

67.   The Founders' Library.

68. The lobby outside the library was originally an open area. Constant demand for efficient use of space has long since turned part of this into an extension of the library for use by the middle school and a room for the use of the mathematics staff.

69. West end of the wing opened in 1934.

70.   The opening of the York Hall in 1934 allowed the former assembly hall to become a well-equipped gymnasium. More than forty years later the opening of the Edinburgh Dome led to its total transformation: divided horizontally, it provided a resources centre with television room and project room at first-floor level. The ground floor is now occupied by classroom W, an office for the Development Director, the bookshop, and an extension to the staff sitting room.

Malvern girls who recalled her charm when, as the 'smiling duchess', she came to open the new wing and plant a copper beech tree—still flourishing—in the quadrangle. Girls, clad in the new uniform of 'champagne beige' summer dresses introduced by Miss Brooks, practised repeatedly the necessary art of curtseying. A special performance of a ballet, choreographed as usual by Miss Phillips, was said to have delighted the royal visitor who was presented with a bouquet of 'college red roses and Scotch heather'. Poor Miss Greenslade was unable to attend the festivities, but a deservedly handsome tribute was paid to her and Miss Poulton as joint Foundresses or joint mothers of the school. Later, their portraits, painted by Keith Henderson and paid for by the Old Girls' Association, were hung in the library. Until the building of the new hall, Speech Day had been held in Malvern's Winter Gardens, the head-mistress' insistence on prior disinfection of the seats resulting in some damp rumps one year. In 1989 the school's increased size made a return to the Winter Gardens necessary, though the contract seems not to include disinfecting the seats!

The financial problems of building the new wing had been solved and the library was an impressive facility for one of the largest girls' schools in the country. But some problems could not be solved, even by the strong wills of Sir Montague Barlow and Miss Iris Brooks. The noise from the railway was sometimes, in those days of steam, very irritating (one wonders how guests at the hotel had coped with it). The Great Western Railway Company was approached with a view to getting the noise stopped. The company was reported in 1934 as being perfectly willing to build a tunnel to confine the noise—provided that the school met most of the £10,000 cost. No more was heard of this scheme, though oral tradition among the staff suggests that Miss Brooks developed her own solution: when a staff meeting was disturbed by a train letting off steam, her secretary was despatched to the station-master and the train was subdued into respectful silence within minutes.

Chapter Six

School Life under Miss Brooks

The summer term of 1938 saw the school with a record number of boarders—426. Only a few years earlier numbers had been so low at 340 that it had been Council policy to encourage more day girls, but in May 1938 this policy was reversed and no new day girls were admitted for some time. Miss Brooks was warmly congratulated on both the high number of boarders and upon the academic achievements of the school—two aspects of her rule which were presumably closely related, since parents were happy to spend money on fees at a school which was reaping such a goodly harvest of awards and places at Oxford and Cambridge, as well as other universities. These distinctions may well explain comments sometimes made by Old Girls of that era who, whilst recognising Miss Brooks' undoubted strengths, lamented that as day-girls they sometimes felt, not merely on the edge of things, but decidedly unwelcome. Another sad phenomenon was the sense of inadequacy that many developed, feeling neglected if they were not academically high-flyers. To provide a school environment which satisfies everybody is impossible: egalitarianism leads to accusations of allowing standards to drop, while excessive competition leads to accusations of not caring for the average pupil. School life under Miss Brooks was colourful and inspiring, but there were some disturbing features, too.

Many views have been expressed of Miss Brooks and her methods of ruling the school. Some people adored her and thought she was great fun, her love of theatricals being but one expression of her sense of fun. Others felt that her love of acting symbolised an insincerity that was intolerable. Her standards must have been difficult to meet: one girl seeking a reference from Miss Brooks was told that she could not make bricks without straw, while another girl quietly doing some non-examination work was told to give up and switch off the light since it was not worth using the electricity for her efforts. Others remembered for years Miss Brooks' wartime assertion that the preservation of great buildings like cathedrals was of more importance than a single human life. Such a philosophy, rating the whole as more important than its constituent parts, explains why several girls remembered any achievement as being recognised for the glory it brought to the school rather than a matter of personal congratulation for the individual. Miss Brooks' own words on Speech Day in 1937 suggest a calculated policy of withholding praise from girls: 'It does not hurt them to be asked sometimes to do hard, uncoaxed, uncomplimented work'. Although Miss Brooks and many of her staff encouraged girls to take part in a wide variety of activities, there is strong evidence to suggest that her pursuit of academic excellence sometimes dried up the well of compassion that distinguishes a loved and respected teacher from one who simply has authority.

Miss Brooks certainly had authority. This was a period when headmistresses wielded enormous power, reinforced by the fact that the appalling casualty rate of the First World War left many women without men to support them in the traditional role of wife and mother. Regardless of inclination, women now needed to undertake paid work, and getting academic qualifications was seen as vital in many families which had happily consigned earlier generations of women to the tasks of supervising home and children. Miss Brooks loved power—some called her 'power-crazy'—and exercised it over her staff as effortlessly as over the girls in an age when the hiring and firing of teachers was unimpeded by modern legislation giving employees rights of tenure and redundancy payments. As late as 1937 the school, in its own magazine, was compared with feudal society, 'based on protection and guidance in return for service and loyalty' with a whiff of a suggestion that the bargain thus struck was a lifetime's commitment.

Nevertheless, certain members of staff stood out as highly individual characters, who made deep and lasting impressions on their pupils, thus underlining the validity of the claim that a school's teachers are much more important than its buildings. One such teacher whose influence was keenly felt was Miss Elinor Jackman, who gave 40 years to the music department of the school, and in 1934 inaugurated the college's own hymnal. She insisted that each girl should own and use a bone-prop, somewhat unhygienically fastened round her neck, and inserted between upper and lower front teeth to keep the mouth open for singing practice! In 1937 the fine for loss of one's bone-prop was said to be an exorbitant half-a-crown, so these instruments of adolescent torture were, in emergency, fashioned out of chalk to avoid Jackie's wrath: she was, though popular, a strict disciplinarian.

A very high standard was maintained in music and drama, the girls' own efforts being encouraged by dedicated teachers and by attending performances by world famous actors and musicians. The entire Birmingham Philharmonic String Orchestra came to the York Hall in 1936 and pupils went to concerts and plays at Malvern Winter Gardens and theatre. During the war years Isobel Baillie, Kathleen Ferrier, Leon Goossens, Myra Hess, Gerald Moore, Moseivitch and many others all came to entertain and inspire the girls. After the war such treats continued: for example, the York Hall was used by the Liverpool Philharmonic Orchestra during the Elgar Festival of 1947 and 'the famous young French cellist, Paul Tortellier, played to us' in 1949. Even those who did not aspire to becoming competent performers themselves learnt from such performances a never-to-be-forgotten lesson—that it is rude to fidget, cough or make the slightest noise when attending a play or concert.

During the 1930s, when the school was building its reputation for excellence and breadth in its teaching, domestic arrangements lagged behind. Growing numbers added urgency to the need to improve accommodation which in some houses was not satisfactory. The Council decided that a proper building policy should be adopted. As their spokesman so accurately put it:

> Buildings have been acquired or leased as the School expanded and necessity arose; nothing like a definite policy of building expansion was ever worked out, nor probably, in view of the rapid growth of the school, and in view also at one period of certain financial difficulties, was it ever possible to do so.

As a building policy began to be formulated, high on the list of priorities was the task of making houses like Summerside and Old Benhams (in Tibberton Road) more attractive and functional. These two were frankly recognised as being unpopular with parents, and so likely to cause the school to lose promising pupils. For some time the school had been keen to acquire the neighbouring Christchurch Vicarage, which was then being let to another tenant. At last (1936-37) it was purchased, and the Council decided to carry out a major building programme there instead of spending large sums on the less suitable Old Benhams. The Vicarage became the Benhams we know today, and a question-mark was to hang over the old house, now usually called Mitchell Lodge, for many years until its eventual demolition in the 1950s. Summerside was also renovated and extended. The bills for these far-reaching

71.   Christchurch Vicarage, much extended, became the new Benhams in January 1939.

72.   The girls' sitting-room in new Benhams. The duties of housemistress were shared by Miss Williams and Miss Warry, who 'made many evenings interesting by her talks on world affairs'—doubtless feeling it wise to prepare her young charges for the troubled times that all responsible adults recognised must lie ahead. 'Awestruck by its newness and magnificence' one of the residents of the new house eulogised about hot and cold water in all the bedrooms and exemption from wearing hats and walking in a crocodile when going to lessons: an unforeseen bonus of moving to a house so close to the main building.

73 & 74.   The new wing of Summerside was opened in the autumn term, 1937. This enabled the house to accommodate 40 girls in the charge of two housemistresses—Miss Spalding and Miss Grayson.

changes and for other work like the new lift in the main building made some worrying dents in the bank balance.

The admission of the first Indian pupil in 1937 was sufficient of an innovation to be mentioned at a Council meeting, it being noted that her brother had been admitted to Malvern College. Girls of foreign extraction were still very much the exception rather than the rule, though many English girls had parents whose work took them abroad, and for whom boarding school offered not simply a good education, but also a stability which would otherwise have been very difficult to achieve. A recurring theme amongst old girls is the value placed upon friendships, often life-long, made at school. Some of these were cemented by the challenge of outwitting staff, an activity in which success was sometimes more apparent than real. Old girls now wonder why midnight feasts were seen as such a triumph when the illicit food was clearly so undesirable, even to palates blunted by boarding school fare: bread and dripping (hidden under the floor-boards) or cakes infested with ants (the tin was buried in the garden) certainly have a rather limited appeal.

The curriculum was very varied and the school was proud of its 'atmosphere of constant activity'. Just as the school today makes provision for girls to study Chinese, in the 1930s the large contingent of girls from South Africa caused Afrikaans to feature on the curriculum—the fact that a member of staff could actually teach this language causing some astonishment. Community service also continued, efforts being particularly focused on St Peter's Home for boys in the Cowleigh Road.

Miss Brooks did considerable teaching herself and made a lasting impression on her pupils. Many still vividly recall her sermons at the Sunday afternoon services which the vicar

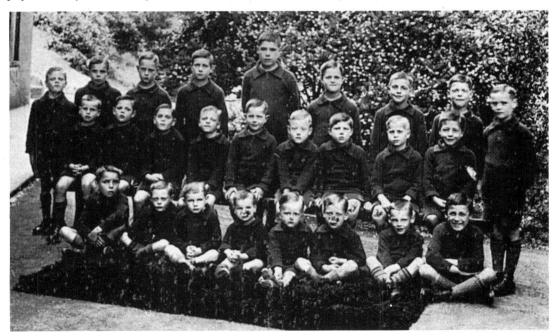

75.   For many years girls took an interest in the welfare of young boys living at St Peter's Home, Cowleigh Road. They arranged outings and other treats for them, though such novelties were firmly forbidden during epidemics of childhood illnessses such as measles, because these were then serious diseases.

76.   Staff ready for Speech Day in the mid-1930s, outside Goodrest. This staff house at the far end of
Victoria Road had an entrance on Graham Road.

of Malvern permitted the school to hold in Malvern Priory church. Her own specialist subject was history but she also had a passion for public speaking and current affairs. Very soon after her arrival the school staged a mock election in 1929, following events in the real national election by means of the 'new valved wireless set' installed in the hall. Not surprisingly, 308 members of the school voted for the Conservative candidate, though the Liberal attracted 48 votes and the Labour 45 votes. Staff dressed as policemen kept order at the polling booths in the quad, quelling college Bolsheviks who fired water pistols at the electorate: such activity suggests a modern approach to teaching and an awareness of international anxiety at the apparent danger posed by communism. The Debating Society was active and in 1933 held a mock League of Nations debate which, according to the chairman of the governors, reached a higher standard than many of the debates he had been obliged to attend at the League's headquarters in Geneva.

It is quite extraordinary that under Miss Brooks' guidance an awareness of current affairs and a training in arts such as that of public speaking flourished alongside a traditionally narrow view of male/female relationships. One of the rules most strictly adhered to was that no girl might speak to a boy: even if she met her own brother in the street, the best attitude for her to adopt was to 'Smile, bow and pass on'. This quaint advice entered the oral and written traditions of the school, generating a little cartoon sketch in the 1938 magazine and also providing the title for Miss Phillips' own eulogy of the Brooks years, published in 1980. On the other hand, there was 'sharp-shooting', which required girls, with virtually no time for preparation, to make a three minute speech on a wide variety of topics. This was intended to encourage a verbal facility, self-confidence and breadth of thought which were curiously at odds with some of the old-fashioned notions about men and boys. Unfortunately, for some girls the experience of making a speech to a highly critical Miss Brooks was something of a trauma, sapping their self-confidence so much that they were unable to open their mouths in public for years. But for others it must have provided an invaluable training and contributed to their achieving distinction in careers such as the law, in which women were breaking new ground.

By the late 1930s ominous clouds were appearing on the horizon and, even in a small town like Malvern, unforeseen changes were about to happen as the names of Mussolini and Hitler began to appear in the newspapers of the world. In 1934 the mother of a German girl had been unable to get money out of Germany; with commendable generosity, despite the financial problems at the school, the Council had decided to let the girl stay, on the understanding that fees would be paid as and when possible.

The school magazine for 1938 contained a topical parody on a Wordsworth sonnet: entitled 'On the Extinction of the Austrian Republic', its theme was the Anschluss by which Hitler forced Austria to unite with Germany in defiance of the peace treaty imposed on Germany at the end of the First World War. The last line, reading 'Thou once great Power, now 'neath a tyrant's hand' is especially interesting—possibly it was Miss Brooks' own teaching that enabled a member of her Upper Sixth to analyse Hitler's character more accurately than the statesmen at Munich managed to do at about the same time.

Surprisingly, even through the turmoil that the tyrant was to cause, the school was able to maintain a remarkable degree of that stability for which so many parents were looking.

Chapter Seven

Evacuation and the Second World War

The First World War had impinged little upon the life of the school though it had occasioned some financial embarrassment among a few parents no longer able to find the fees. But the Second World War and preparations for it caused an immediate and major disruption, for the school buildings in Malvern had to be evacuated. The authorities in Whitehall, anticipating war, earmarked Malvern as a safe retreat to which it might be necessary to remove the government. Nearby, Madresfield Court would have become the home of the royal family, while the spacious and sprawling buildings of both Malvern College and Malvern Girls' College could quite easily be adapted to a number of purposes. Among the belated Christmas greetings received in the mail on Boxing Day 1938 by Miss Brooks and Mr. Gaunt, headmaster of the boys' college, were the unseasonable tidings that, in the event of war, they would have to find, possibly within 48 hours, alternative accommodation for their pupils and staff. Even this advance notice was of limited use, for two reasons. Firstly, despite all those anxious months during which Hitler made more and more outrageous demands, no-one could predict precisely when, or even if, war would occur; secondly, the notification of the government's contingency plans carried strict instructions that close secrecy must be maintained. Finding alternative accommodation for several hundred people was a difficult enough task in itself; to do so at the same time as observing the secrecy so vital for the country's security was well-nigh impossible. But both heads, with considerable tenacity and a certain measure of good fortune, managed to find satisfactory solutions. The boys and their staff spent the 1939-40 academic year at Blenheim Palace and then, after a brief respite back at Malvern, were exiled for a longer period at Harrow from 1942 until 1946, while their college was used for the scientific research that was to make a major contribution to the Allied victory. The girls were more fortunate: they experienced only one year of evacuation, but did encounter the problems of being split into three separate groups. But at least they all went to the same county—Somerset.

Miss Brooks with her close friend and secretary, Miss Grace Phillips, spent several weeks and a good deal of energy seeking out suitable accommodation. Each of the three houses which were eventually taken was set in its own parkland in rural Somerset. Even today, half a century later, their settings remain idyllic despite the inevitable changes which have occurred to and around them. The only house which the college actually bought was Horsington House, which was to hold the 70 girls in the Junior School under the supervision of Miss Watson, who devoted a total of 34 years to the school from 1922 until 1956. For £6,000 the school acquired not only the attractive house, but also the stables, garages, lodge and three cottages, together with 20 acres. After the war this house became a Dr. Barnardo Home, eventually being sold for use as an hotel in the 1970s.

Two other houses were rented. The Middle School, numbering 70 girls, went to Brymore, birthplace of John Pym, the man who so memorably defied Charles I. It was still the home of the Pym family in the 1930s. Miss Dellow took charge of the Middle School girls here, and

77.   During the 1939-40 evacuation 70 girls in the Junior School went to Horsington House in Somerset.

78.   The Middle School went to Brymore, in the care of Miss Dellow.

their adaptation of the house as a school seemed to set something of a precedent: in 1952 the house was sold to Somerset County Council for use once more as a school. It remains a most unusual educational institution as a school for 150 boarders and 50 day pupils who receive an all-round education with particular emphasis on agricultural training. Situated at Cannington, four miles from Bridgwater, Brymore was taken by Malvern Girls' College for a three year period at a rent of £600 a year but, as events turned out, was used by the school for only one year.

Miss Brooks took the 150 older girls, from the Lower Fifth upwards, to Hinton House, rented at £1,000 a year from the 8th Earl Poulett. Miss Phillips has written at some length about the experiences of those responsible for organising the evacuation to Hinton St George. Lord Poulett was to prove a most helpful landlord, though he was initially somewhat uncooperative and understandably put out by the invasion of females shattering the rural tranquillity of his lifestyle. An eminently practical man, he was mistaken by some girls for the local handyman as he worked tirelessly at installing electrical circuits and carrying out other maintenance on the huge mansion that was his home. But, despite his best endeavours, girls remember that winter as bitterly cold, when their face-cloths froze into hardened shapes overnight in the wash-basins. When Malvern Girls' College left Hinton in 1940 it was temporarily occupied by another school which presumably found similar problems. Many years later, in 1973, Lord Poulett died without direct heir, having made arrangements that the house should be sold. It has since been divided into several homes occupied by different families. This really is the only way that a building designed for an earlier and grander way of life can now be maintained and used for its original purpose—as home. After the war Malvern Girls' College retained a reminder of the Somerset interlude in the use of Poulett family names—Amias, Hercules, John and Vere—for Sixth Form sitting rooms in the main building.

Several staff and girls have recorded their experiences of the evacuation. In August 1939 some staff and day-girls came into school to help with the organisation and packing preparatory to leaving Malvern. Warwick House, the high-class store which closed in 1992 after 159 years of trading in the town, was once known as Cox and Painter's and had a removals department, so naturally its help was enlisted. The school's loyal house staff like Stainer the caretaker and Oliver the chauffeur also played vital roles. As Miss Brooks herself wrote:

79.   The exterior of the grand house at Hinton St George, as it was at the beginning of this century.

to Brymore—though some thousands of pickled eggs, carefully preserved according to school tradition, had to be disposed of! Fifty tons of furniture destined for the 50 rooms of Brymore arrived in a constant stream lasting four days. Brymore's owner had been insistent that he would stay, with his five dogs and parrot, but when, as Miss Dellow put it, the 'tide of furniture washed up to the doors' of his rooms, he fled. Brymore had to be modernised for use by the college: an air-raid shelter, bathrooms, plumbing, extra lighting, heating and cooking facilities were the first priorities. A gymnasium was created in a garage, a laboratory in a harness room and a 'music corridor' in the five-roomed flat formerly occupied by the chauffeur and situated over the stables. Even a studio was established, using the former laundry of the house, while hockey, netball and lacrosse pitches were sited on neighbouring land. Its owner, a local farmer, even fitted up 'on a large oak tree, a wonderful contraption of planks and wire, for the accommodation of our seventy blazers and sweaters'.

There were obvious practical problems in the way of keeping the school united during the evacuation, because Brymore and Horsington were each over twenty miles from Hinton St George—one to the north-west and the other to the north-east! Such problems, however, were minor compared with the problems facing the country itself: France fell to the Germans and Hitler stood poised to add Britain to the list of countries brought under Nazi domination, while the school lived an unreal existence in its three rural retreats. Several old girls have particularly vivid memories of that time and its excitements: for the younger girls there were lessons in Horsington's music room, with its gilding, chandeliers and a reputation of being haunted! For the seniors, Hinton was even more grand, though the promise of sleeping in the earl or the countess's room lost some appeal with the realisation that the honour was to be shared with numerous others, for each room had become a dormitory. Beauty was all around, both indoors and out, especially at Hinton. The house was full of paintings, tapestries and other antiques, while the surrounding gardens and parkland did much to uplift the spirits of girls and staff who inevitably worried about what was happening in the world outside. Miss Brooks issued daily news bulletins for the girls, but never allowed them to see the anxiety which she, like so many others, must have been suffering at that desperate time. Some girls recall seeing British Spitfires fighting overhead with German aircraft, while school lessons went on as normally as possible; biology and art in Brymore's stable courtyard became particularly memorable as the scent of wisteria wafted through the air. Some time was spent helping on local farms—seen as a more practical and productive means of getting physical exercise than the games lessons which were accordingly reduced. Amid all the national anxiety of 1940 came the good news for the school that Ivydene Hall, Beaufort, Avenue, Lindfield, the new Benhams and Hatley St George would not be required by the government, and that most of the other school buildings, including the vital main building at the old *Imperial Hotel*, would also be released. As with Malvern (boys') College, however, the authorities reserved the right to issue a notice to vacate them within 48 hours if they were needed for some vital war purpose. Even with this proviso, it was decided to try to get back to normal, everyone returning to Malvern in the autumn of 1940. Pupil numbers had dwindled in the autumn of 1939 to about 300, reflecting the national mood of uncertainty as to what the future might hold, and the desire of many parents to keep their children with them in such distressing times. The enormous cost of the evacuation had been in part met by the £4,000 paid as compensation when the government took over the school and by the sale of the Golf House, but now £1,200 had to be found to provide air-raid shelters in Malvern. Nevertheless, none of the usual appeals went out to parents; Miss Brooks, in particular, felt it unwise to do 'anything that might tend to discourage parents at the present time.' She was probably right; in any event, numbers rose dramatically to 440 when the school returned to Malvern, and had an astonishing 475 boarders and 59 day boarders by the spring of 1943.

No school magazines appeared during the war years, presumably due more to the national paper shortage than to reluctance to produce them. Rationing naturally caused some difficulty, not least over school uniform, former pupils being urged to return their coats and other items for resale—the first time that the school actively encouraged the sale of secondhand uniform. The School Council minutes of this period do not contain much comment on the precarious position of Britain but it is interesting to note the order from the local fire brigade to keep the swimming bath full, and the concern as to the best method to camouflage so large a building as the old *Imperial Hotel* as protection from air attack. A suggestion that flower pots filled with shrubs should be placed on the flat roof of the York Hall extension was about the best idea to emerge! Meanwhile, at Brymore, the 'Dig for Victory' campaign had very tangible success: 'the military' rented the grounds to grow crops, and the school itself received over ten tons of fruit and vegetables.

The momentous events of the war years eclipsed more domestic concerns that might otherwise have been observed more fittingly. On 30 September 1940 Miss Poulton celebrated her 90th birthday, an occasion which Miss Greenslade survived by only 11 days. Her funeral in the priory church was rather a desolate affair: Miss Poulton, in her businesslike way, seems to have left instructions for her own funeral which took place in Christ Church, Avenue Road, in the summer of 1942 though part of the florist's bill was unfortunately overlooked by the school governors!

Chapter Eight

The Winds of Change

In her prime Miss Brooks had been regarded as a progressive headmistress, but by the 1950s she had held power for over twenty years and it was felt in some quarters that a younger woman, with more modern ideas and a more flexible attitude, was needed. Schools can be indelibly stamped by the characters of their heads: in periods of change or uncertainty at the top a school merely ticks over, the staff probably still giving of their best but, each with his or her own skills and beliefs, unable to perform with the same effectiveness as is possible when efforts are co-ordinated and led by a decisive hand. Malvern Girls' College owes much of its high reputation to strong, positive leadership by women of character. Happy accident produced a Miss Poulton or a Miss Brooks at the time that the climate of opinion needed them, and Miss Brooks certainly ensured that Malvern Girls' College won wide acclaim for academic excellence

81.   Music has been one of the school's strengths from the earliest days. Here, the school orchestra is shown in rehearsal for a broadcast given in the Midland Regional Children's Hour on 24 July 1947—a day of great excitement. Music was the bond on another exciting day soon after the boys of Malvern College returned from their wartime evacuation to Harrow: the girls' orchestra gave a concert at the Boys' College, and the hope was expressed in the Malvern Girls' College magazine that this might 'be the beginning of many similar shared pleasures'. Fraternising with the boys was still not encouraged, but it was clearly no longer practical to retain the rule requiring girls to 'Smile, bow and pass on' if they met one of this dangerous species.

and for the breadth of its teaching. Her opinionated and self-righteous attitude fitted in well at a time when the new woman of the '30s was in the slightly eccentric mould of Muriel Spark's Miss Jean Brodie, whose prime was so vividly encapsulated in the highly acclaimed screen performance of Maggie Smith. But such women ran risks: they alienated many and they undermined the self-esteem of weaker pupils, a fact which is sadly clear from the comments of several less academic Malvern Old Girls of the 1930s and 1940s. Furthermore, when they and their methods became old-fashioned—unsuited to the more egalitarian ideas which were to emerge in the post-war period—they lacked the flexibility to adapt to necessary change in method and approach.

Miss Brooks' retirement in 1954 marked the end of an era in college history, enabling the Council to appoint Miss Margaret Burgess as the reforming head seen by many to be needed at this point. In the 14 years of her headship Miss Burgess left a permanent mark on the school, seeing through not only practical changes in its organisation but very significant changes in attitude. Her common sense, kindness and understanding of human nature brought about much greater flexibility, and the expression 'happy atmosphere' started to be used by visitors describing their impressions on entering the school. Miss Brooks had run a very tight ship, retaining personal direction of every aspect of school life, from producing the time-table of every teacher and pupil in the school to supervising the school's domestic arrangements. Miss Burgess, who had extensive teaching and administrative experience before coming to Malvern, saw the virtues of delegating areas of responsibility to able and experienced members of her staff, a policy which was not easy to instigate, particularly since Miss Brooks left behind staff who were fiercely defensive of all that she had stood for. The innovations yielded enormous benefits in the longer term and proved especially valuable in 1967-68, the last year of Miss Burgess' headship when, worn out by the exertions of the changes she had initiated, she was physically unable to go on any longer and the school functioned perfectly well in the hands of her admirable deputy, Miss Mary Micklewright.

In Miss Burgess the college, already enjoying a reputation for very high academic standards, acquired for the first time a graduate scientist as headmistress. Perhaps that is why, under her leadership and with the enthusiastic work of Miss Margaret Jago as head of Science, Malvern Girls' College came to be seen as that exceptional institution—a girls' school with a reputation for excellence in scientific subjects. In 1956 it was the first girls' school to qualify for a £10,000 grant from the

82.   Miss Iris Brooks retired in 1954. This photograph of her hangs in the Founders' Library. She died, aged 77, in 1971.

83 & 84.   Parkfield, in Victoria Road, was somewhat distant from the main building. Miss Temperley was well able to run it as a virtually separate preparatory department. Both the formal group photograph and the children at leisure were taken in 1949.

Industrial Fund for the Advancement of Scientific Education in Schools, thus laying the foundations for the reorganisation of the entire science department and the building of the essential new biology block adjacent to the York Hall.

Miss Burgess had inherited a school excellent in many ways but very much due for overhaul in others. Since some problems impinged upon others, a combination of factors led to boarding arrangements, teaching facilities and admissions policy being reformed simultaneously in the early 1960s, producing a lasting effect on several aspects of school life.

Central to the changes was the recognition that it was not desirable for the main building to provide boarding facilities for some Upper Fifths in School House as well as the Sixth Formers in Senior House. This practice caused the latter to lose something of their special identity and, perhaps more seriously, the Middle School houses to lose some of their natural leaders. For the individual there was the perennial question—which girls were to be siphoned off from their Middle School houses and placed in the main building?

At the lower end of the school there were other difficulties to be solved in the junior departments housed in Hatley St George and in Parkfield, which had ceased to house the domestic science department during the war. From 1946 Parkfield had accepted girls from the

85.   An aerial view taken in 1955 by Ann Tempest. It clearly shows the contrasting architectural styles of the main building.

age of six, the intention being that they would spend four years in what was effectively a separate preparatory school under the capable direction of Miss Edna Temperley, who had joined the school in 1929. At the age of 10 they would go on to spend a year in Hatley and were then guaranteed a place in Malvern Girls' College to the end of their school career, which thus spanned a total of at least ten years and often considerably longer. By the late 1950s, however, fewer parents were interested in boarding schools for little girls but did want them for their adolescent daughters. Recognising the high reputation of Malvern Girls' College and the difficulty of securing a place, they found that there was a simple means of ensuring entry for their daughters—send them to the preparatory department at the age of ten. This course of action is not in the least surprising, but it produced several problems for the school. It meant that the junior departments were top-heavy, catering in the main for 10-year-olds, whilst the college itself lost control of choice of entrants. Furthermore, girls who had formed friendships in the junior department sought to enter specific middle school houses together and, although the school tried to meet these requests, it could not always do so. By about 1960 Parkfield and Hatley St George needed a good deal of money to be spent on repairs and modernisation, while both Miss Temperley and her deputy were due to retire.

This multiplicity of problems was not easy to solve. Miss Burgess herself cut the Gordian knot by suggesting to the Council that a new middle school house should be built. Hatfield was born, built to a novel design on college land a stone's throw from the main building. The

86.   Many pupils became brownies or guides. This picture was taken in 1956 at Hatley St George.

87.   Hatfield in 1964.

school magazine in 1963 commented that the 'hexagons of the new house are taking shape where once we picked raspberries and gooseberries'. The somewhat distant accommodation for the juniors at Hatley St George and Parkfield was sold but the name 'Hatfield' preserves a syllable from each of these original houses. The decisions of this period effected an important change in the admission policy of the school, which ceased to cater for girls below the age of eleven.

Miss Burgess saw through not only the building of Hatfield but also major changes in the use of the main building. In these plans she was encouraged by the school's governing Council and especially by Mrs. Arthur Gibbs who had joined the Council in 1940 and was to become its chairman in 1964. As chairman of the House Committee she worked hard at trying to make school buildings more comfortable and attractive. The new middle school house enabled all Upper Fifths to be removed from boarding accommodation in the main building, allowing bedrooms and sitting rooms on school corridor to be turned into classrooms. At last all teaching could be carried on in the main building, encouraging a sense of unity as well as improving efficiency. The mysterious basement area was opened up to become the senior dining room with adjacent up-to-date kitchens; the former dining room at the front of the college became the senior common room. Capped and aproned serving maids disappeared, as did trolleys bearing tepid food on circuitous routes around the building. Self-service canteen facilities arrived here at about the same time as self-service supermarkets caught on in the outside world, and everyone agreed on how much more convenient and comfortable it all was.

Under the enlightened leadership of Miss Burgess changes occurred also in staffing. When she had arrived in 1954 most full-time teaching staff were resident, as they had been

88. Miss Brooks was succeeded by Miss Margaret Burgess, seen here, left, with Mrs. Arthur Gibbs on Speech Day.

required to be until 1951. They either took charge of boarding houses or lived in one of the houses—Abbotsmead, Standish or the delightfully named Goodrest in Graham Road—which the school had acquired and adapted over many years for communal use by staff. It hardly needs to be said that no man featured in these arrangements. At a time when the winds of change were blowing vigorously through state schools, causing the virtual demise of the old grammar schools and the mushroom growth of co-educational comprehensive schools, Miss Burgess recognised that her school needed to let in a breath of fresh air, too. She appointed several non-resident teachers, some of them male. The government scientific establishment, which came as the Telecommunications Research Establishment in 1942 and is now known as the Defence Research Agency, in bringing highly qualified scientists to Malvern also brought their equally qualified spouses: from the 1960s until the present the school has chosen many of its non-resident staff from this rich pool of talent. Miss Burgess also appointed non-teaching housemistresses—a particularly courageous step along a path strewn with traps for the unwary.

Traditionally, the housemistresses in girls' boarding schools had been senior members of the teaching staff who had taken on additional responsibility in the houses for a meagre increase in salary. It was a heavy burden, 24 hours a day throughout the term and often beyond. Some of these necessarily unmarried women were superb at the pastoral care of their charges while others were, to put it gently, less gifted in this field. Miss Burgess saw that the appointment of non-teachers as housemistresses presented distinct possibilities of improved relationships and performance in both the house and the classroom. She was one of the first to recognise the importance of a good housemistress and to experience the difficulties in securing the services of suitable candidates for posts which had for too long been underrated and underpaid. The governing Council of the school began to recognise the problem soon after

89.   The Senior Dining Room in 1962.

90.   The Senior Common Room in 1962.

Miss Burgess was appointed—doubtless she had some part in the hopes that they expressed in 1956 that the living quarters of housemistresses could soon be improved. Even so, considerable hurdles clearly remained: in the mid-1960s one unfortunate house had seven different house-mistresses in less than two years.

It was not until 1967 that the position of housemistress of Senior House was separated from that of headmistress, at long last freeing the head from the onerous task of day-to-day organisation. The close interweaving of Senior House and school administration was, of course, a legacy from the past: its much-needed separation was another break from the authoritarian methods of Miss Brooks. Similarly, whilst Miss Brooks felt herself able to advise all her pupils on their future careers, Miss Burgess saw the need for specialist help and appointed a careers adviser for the older girls. In more recent years this work, together with advice on applications for further education, has been greatly expanded and is now a vital part of the school's preparation of girls to play their rightful role in the egalitarian world of business and other careers.

In addition to the obvious and tangible changes in the main building, there were other changes which led to greater efficiency, not least the installation of an internal telephone exchange in 1968. This led to a great saving of time and energy—as anyone who has had to find an individual in this vast building will confirm. A full-time librarian was appointed in 1964, the Council recognising that the work was far too much for a member of the teaching staff to cope with in addition to teaching commitments.

By the mid-1960s, girls were becoming increasingly involved in the world outside school: 40 girls embarked in 1966 on the early Duke of Edinburgh award schemes and both judo and driving lessons became available at about the same time. There was a growing awareness of the desirability of mixing with other schools in the area, but the spectre of boy-girl relation-ships prevented much headway being made in this new policy. Nevertheless, when Miss Veronica Owen took up the headship in 1968 the school was, in her own words, a thoroughly progressive and modern school. The Council, too, paid tribute to Miss Burgess who 'had done great work for the College, brought it up to date and stream-lined its running'.

Its sound reputation in science teaching made it an unusual school for girls and it soon revealed a desire to break another old-fashioned mould: plans began to ensure that the girls, products of quite privileged families (at least in financial terms), should become more conscious of the problems and lifestyles of those far less generously endowed with material benefits. For example, 18 children from Peckham in London and 20 from the urban area of Winson Green proved valuable eye-openers when they came to the college for summer holidays in 1970 and 1971. Community service had, since the 1930s, involved helping the inmates of local chil-dren's homes—St Peter's and St Edward's in Malvern, the Good Shepherd in Hanley Swan and St Mary's in Eastnor, seven miles away. But under the gently mocking eye of the tireless Miss June Roundhill, encouraged by Miss Owen, the work was expanded to include care for the elderly, the handicapped and the deprived not only locally, but also in London, Birming-ham, Coventry and other big towns. This has remained an important feature of college life ever since. All Lower Sixth girls now undertake a week's Community Service, mostly away from school; it was soon recognised as a very effective way of ensuring that they learn a good deal about the realities of life in a wide variety of fields.

Miss Owen, like Miss Burgess, was a headmistress who brought a wider vision of the needs which the school might satisfy. During her headship a greater proportion of foreign girls was welcomed. Miss Owen believes that increased applications from foreign girls which occurred at about the same time as her arrival were circumstantial. This is too modest: with her long experience of education in Kenya, and conscious of the problems of emergent nations, Miss Owen was aware of the advantages which could be gained through the cultural and educational intercourse which resulted from opening Malvern's doors to foreign students. A woman of wisdom—one Old Girl remarked 'How wise those eyes always seemed to be'—and of wide experience, yet totally lacking the social pretensions of many in her position, she recognised that the benefits were by no means one way. The high standards demanded by, for example, the African or Chinese, together with the introduction of some of the culture of other societies could help and enrich the school quite as much as the school helped the foreign student. Economically, too, the increased demand from foreign students for places was good news for the school at this time when, for several reasons, the number of applications from girls in this country fell. A very significant cause of this was a climate of opinion in the 1960s hostile to the independent schools and their social divisiveness. It was the age of the new equality, the comprehensive school and the throwing out of old traditions as Harold Wilson's government lurched from one economic problem to another and tried to change British society after what it constantly referred to as 'thirteen wasted years of Tory misrule'.

At the same time as these changes were occurring in Britain, former British colonies were losing, as part of the winds of change within the Commonwealth, the traditional British education which had been a strong feature for several generations. Furthermore, political conflict and upheaval turned parts of, for example, Africa into trouble spots where children could become victims of civil strife. A British education was held in high regard so a significant number of foreign parents wanted to send their children to be educated in Britain, insisting that these young people should seize every opportunity presented to them by the school. Some of these parents worked for the United Nations or in the embassies of their own countries and many had themselves been educated in Britain. The motivation and hard work of such pupils resulted in high standards of achievement for many of them and, rather unexpectedly perhaps, they helped to raise the standard aimed at by less motivated or less able girls born in the British Isles, for the latter determined not to be put to shame by foreigners who had the in-built disadvantages caused by language and cultural differences. At her first Speech Day in 1969 Miss Owen—an exciting and interesting new personality—spoke of how valuable it was for the young to learn naturally as they worked together that everyone, whatever their nationality or colour, had a unique contribution to make: 'If a defence of the independent boarding school was needed this by itself seemed enough.'

A further significant change was made in the appointment of housemistresses. Miss Owen agreed with Miss Burgess, seeing the role of housemistress as too important to be tacked on to an already demanding job. She also recognised the benefits of introducing into the boarders' environment an element of family life which had hitherto been missing and, with the Council's support, tried to provide for newly appointed housemistresses accommodation that would enable them to bring a husband, children and even pets into a building that became over the years more and more like home to successive generations of schoolgirls. Today, middle and senior school houses are in the care of women who are picked for their interest in pastoral care of the young rather than their position in the league of academic responsibility or their need to earn a living after the loss of a husband. Some are married, some are not; some have grown up children and some have families so young that they take maternity leave to increase them. Some, but not all, are on the teaching staff in a part-time capacity but all maintain strong links with what goes on in the academic life of the school. To many girls their housemistress becomes a term-time mother to whom they turn even after leaving school. The separation of the role of housemistress from that of teacher was therefore an important one, greatly extending

91.   The Edinburgh Dome.

the field of candidates from which appointments may be made in this vital aspect of boarding school life.

One particularly visible change during Miss Owen's headship was marked by the opening on Ascension Day 1978 by the Duke of Edinburgh of the dome named after him. Unconventional in design, it had aroused considerable interest during its construction, especially on Ascension Day in May 1977 when, the weather being especially co-operative, it was inflated amidst great excitement. Its completion emphasised the recognition of the importance of physical education, which has always been a strength of the school: 10 years earlier the swimming bath had been deepened and modernised so that it could be used throughout the year. Malvern Girls' College entered the 1980s with superb indoor facilities for sports and gymnastics and soon added outdoor all-weather pitches too.

The dome can also be used for worship, dance, music and drama. In addition it enabled the school to forge closer links with the town because the Bionics Club, organised by the girls, soon became a much appreciated means by which local physically handicapped adults could enjoy sports and games in the dome. The opening of the dome freed the former gymnasium in the main building for numerous purposes. The top half was blocked off, providing a television and project room—the nucleus of the Resources Centre started by the late Dr. David Sidebottom in 1976. The extensive ground floor space has been adapted into a new classroom, accommodation for the Development Director appointed in 1991, a sitting-room for staff and, thanks to the generosity of Miss Owen, a paperback bookshop where girls can browse and buy books within a termly budget set individually by their parents. In its first week the shop sold 400 books! Elmslie, the original architect of the *Imperial Hotel*, might well turn in his grave at this latest use of his vast and majestic room which has served so many purposes: coffee-room, ballroom, assembly hall, gymnasium. However this room, through its many refurbishments, has certainly been known, loved and used by countless people.

Since Miss Brooks' departure there had been changes on the academic front. The secretarial department had been abolished in 1958 and certain other subjects, like classics, had been under threat because, attracting relatively small classes, they were considered expensive to staff. The solution to this particular problem was found in a policy which Miss Brooks would have found difficult to accept: some classes were shared with the boys of Malvern College. Girls and boys could at last, with the blessing of the authorities, enter each other's schools!

Academic standards were never allowed to slip but, as Her Majesty's Inspectors were told when they descended in force for a general inspection in 1974, the school continued to cater for a wider range of ability than was usually found in the traditional grammar schools. Very academically able girls were not creamed off: 'we hope to assess in the work of an eleven year old the ability to take five subjects at Ordinary Level and then expect her to be able to achieve more than that as a result of small classes, experienced teaching and an atmosphere of disciplined work.' This recipe certainly seemed to work, for academic success went hand-in-hand with a happy atmosphere. One preparatory school head wrote:

92. Miss Owen at Commemoration 1979 with guest of honour Dame Elizabeth Lane, the first woman high court judge and one of the school's most distinguished old girls. Also in the picture are Professor Bryan Brooke (right), chairman of the school's governing Council 1972-82, and Mr. John Frith, current chairman.

93.   Miss Veronica Owen.

I have always admired the way that the school seems to look at each girl as a whole, and is not only interested in what she can put down on paper, but in what she is like as a person as well. I remember how unhappy A.B. was before coming to you, and how quickly she seemed to become part of the school and happy again. I never felt that C.D. was particularly gifted academically, but she seems to have made a niche for herself and done well with you, while her younger sister has had the opportunity to continue with her music, and also writes extremely happily.

This letter, with its reference to the musical life of the school, was written shortly before the formation of the Jenny Lind Singers in 1970. The group, created to sing Swedish songs at Malvern's celebration of the 150th anniversary of the birth of Jenny Lind, has won international acclaim—though not yet quite on the scale of the singer after whom it is named! The 'Swedish Nightingale' spent the last years of her life in Malvern, living in a house called Wynd's Point, close to the great hill known as the British Camp or Herefordshire Beacon. She is buried in Malvern cemetery.

Miss Owen's appointment came towards the end of what is often referred to as 'the swinging sixties' when traditional ideas and values were increasingly questioned. The school was very fortunate in having a head with the ability to move with the times and yet keep a firm grip on traditional values. For example, she gave girls greater freedom of which one symbol was the abolition of school uniform for the Sixth Form, a decision which delighted them but raised the eyebrows of many in the ranks of Old Girls and local inhabitants. But she was unswerving in her insistence on adherence to any school rule that she saw as vital to the maintenance of unity and goodwill within the community. One might mutter about the thwarting of a plan one had conceived, but one never doubted for an instant that if Miss Owen said 'No' she had asked herself the simple question, 'What is best for the community?'.

The 30 years following Miss Brooks' retirement had seen a good deal of change in both attitudes and school facilities. The launching of Polygon in 1972 gave the girls a forum to express their opinions, the first exciting trips to the U.S.S.R., organised by the history department, were offered to senior girls and the school bought its first computer. These three examples, chosen at random, reflect how much society was changing: the generation which is now in its 50s witnessed the changes without immediately recognising their impact. The generation which had been expected to obey its elders and betters became the one which had to listen to its own children and Polygon reflected that trend; Russia, mysterious and sinister, grudgingly admitting tourists to its lands behind the Iron Curtain, is now exposed for the world to see; and a school without a good array of computers, televisions, video machines and other technological wonders is seen as lacking basic essentials.

Chapter Nine

Malvern Girls' College Today

The school had a difficult period when Miss Owen retired, one unfortunate intake of pupils experiencing no fewer than four headmistresses in as many years. The ill-health of Mrs. Eileen Stamers-Smith prevented her ever really getting into her stride as headmistress, though she initiated some changes such as the provision of better accommodation for both girls and staff. In view of her age and lack of recent full-time teaching experience, her appointment by the Council was surprising. Her short headship certainly served to highlight the enormous demands made on a headmistress in the 1980s and the months that followed her premature departure saw the Council taking careful stock of the situation. They, and the school, were very fortunate in having loyal and experienced staff whose strength ensured that the inevitable difficulties were overcome.

94.   Mrs. Eileen Stamers-Smith.

Invaluable at this critical time was Miss Delmé Moore who had first come to the school in 1947, staying for five years. Returning in 1957, she took charge of the mathematics department, served as Senior Mistress and then took over as Deputy Headmistress when Miss Micklewright retired in 1973. She had looked forward to retirement in 1985 but, with her long experience, agreed to take on the headship until a suitable permanent appointment could be made. Dr. Valerie Payne, who had joined the school to teach physics in 1969, served as her deputy and eventually took up the headship in 1986.

When school governors appoint new heads they usually look for new blood in order to ensure that a school does not stagnate, so there was some surprise that Malvern Girls' College decided to appoint a teacher who had already spent nearly twenty years at the school. Some years on, it is now possible to see that it is not necessary to have a new broom to sweep clean. Dr. Payne became head at a critical period in the history of the school and a time of educational upheaval in this country. Her intimate knowledge of the school proved to be a valuable stabilising force: she was a vital link between the old and the new when the school was adapting to the greatest changes seen in the educational world for decades.

Whilst independent schools have been spared much of the unease which embittered and worried the maintained sector, they had to meet the challenge of the introduction of the General Certificate of Secondary Education. The old General Certificate of Education had been introduced in 1950: many teachers felt that a new approach was overdue and welcomed the changes brought about by G.C.S.E. But undoubtedly teachers throughout the country found their workload much increased as they took a fresh look at teaching methods, thinking very carefully indeed about how they needed to adjust to preparing candidates for public examinations which were very different from those which had been set for nearly forty years.

The educational world of the 1980s and 1990s has also been much exercised by the National Curriculum proposals, involving core subjects which all pupils must study, and a selection of others based on the inclination of pupils and teachers. Whilst independent schools do not have to follow all government recommendations they would be extremely shortsighted if they completely turned their backs on developments brought about by changing educational thought or even government policy. The debates which have raged nationwide over curriculum, staff appraisal and pupil profiling have naturally made their impact on this school. In addition, the 1989 Children Act had particular implications for boarding schools. On top of all this, modern thinking emphasises the need for improved communication between staff, pupils and parents. Such changes have meant that the traditional role of headmasters and headmistresses has been very much broadened—it has become too heavy a burden for even the most dedicated to shoulder alone.

Dr. Payne applied the objective eye of the scientist to the daunting task that faced her. Having immersed herself in the new science of management she began a programme of change and democratisation which was not universally popular but proved to be very effective. She soon set up a management structure giving increased responsibility for specific areas of school administration to certain members of staff. A key aspect of this was the institution of staff heads of the lower middle school, upper middle school and sixth form. Each was given responsibility comparable to that formerly exercised by a headmistress, though, of course, it was necessary for her as headmistress to retain overall control. This delegation showed both her awareness of growing trends in the business world and a certain prescience, comparable to that of the school's founders, as to where the educational world was going. For example, the development of pupil profiling and the need for increasingly detailed references when girls leave school necessitated some division of responsibility. Not even the all-knowing and robust Miss Brooks could have coped with the workload imposed by today's demands.

Another important aspect of school life was the so-called 'shape of the day'. During the winter and spring terms the school had, since time immemorial, had academic lessons in the mornings and in the evenings, from 4.30 until 6.30, leaving the afternoons free for games and other activities. Evening lessons were felt by many staff and pupils to be very unsatisfactory: people were tired and, as one member of staff put it, 'I find it very unnatural to be teaching exhausted twelve year olds with the moon shining through the window'. The shape of the day was hotly debated and, after extensive discussion and investigation, Dr. Payne decided to change it. This was a major break with the past, felt by most to be desperately needed, but opposed by others. The headmistress did not immediately earn universal approval, but few now would question the benefits her decision brought. The change enabled teaching of academic subjects to end at 4 p.m. and opened up the possibility of a wide variety of activities during the period from tea-time until supper-time at 7 p.m. Whilst it was breaking with one of the school's traditions,

95. Miss C. Delmé Moore.

it was very much in line with another—the provision of a good all-round education. Adaptability is a recurring theme in all institutions which have stood the test of time. The shape of the day may not arouse much interest outside Malvern Girls' College, but has had far-reaching effects within it and provides an excellent example of the beneficial effects of being adaptable.

Recent years have seen the school constantly updating its facilities. Old-fashioned rooms with wasted dark corners have, for example, been transformed into a modern well-equipped computer centre. The school's governing body is in control of the school's finances and strives to ensure a fair allocation of its resources. The demands in a boarding school are even greater than in a day-school—so the Council has to balance not simply the needs of a wide diversity of subjects in the curriculum, but also the domestic and

96. Greenslade.

material comforts of those who board in the college.

The opening of Greenslade, the new senior house, named after one of the school's founders, marked a continuing improvement in boarding facilities. Opened in 1988, it increased the accommodation for sixth formers who had hitherto lived in the main building in conditions which by modern standards had become quite unsatisfactory. Far too cramped and lacking in privacy, the old accommodation may have encouraged some senior girls to leave at the end of their upper fifth year, though in fact they sometimes went to boys' schools which had decided to accept girls into their sixth forms and had even less desirable provision for girls. The building of Greenslade and the refurbishment of accommodation in the main building gave seniors a choice of two pleasant houses. They can either live in the modern purpose built Greenslade, seen by many as akin to a well-equipped hotel, at a decent

97. Dr. Valerie Payne.

distance from the main teaching area of the school; or they can choose to make themselves at home in Poulton, conveniently close to the library and other school facilities such as music rooms. Each year, as girls enter the sixth form, they debate the relative merits of each: most find it a very difficult decision. But then, they are about to face much more harrowing choices when they leave the protection of school.

An interesting and useful innovation has been the institution of the Sixth Form Council—not, of course, to be confused with the school's governing Council. The Sixth Form Council reflects the school's belief that girls of this age are young adults who should participate in formulating the philosophy and rules of the society in which they live. Any sixth former whose behaviour is deemed to have brought the good name of the school into disrepute is required to appear before this council, consisting of both sixth formers and staff; after consideration of the circumstances she may be required by her peers to change her ways and undergo some punishment such as gating for a weekend—or the discussion may have opened up some feature of school life which is in need of change. The headmistress, of course, still deals directly with any major breach of discipline.

At Malvern Girls' College the individual needs of pupils are seen as extremely important, the headmistress and staff being acutely aware that a boarding school has particular responsibility to ensure that any talent or skill should be developed. When asked to say what, above all else, she would like the school to give its pupils, Dr. Payne is quite unequivocal: self-esteem. This is encouraged by building upon any natural aptitude and it gives girls the confidence to make choices during and subsequent to their school careers. If it may be argued that a school fails whenever any pupil leaves with no sense of purpose, then this school, which sends out young women with a proper sense of self-respect and direction, is doing remarkably well. Like the founders in the 1890s, today's headmistress can have no realistic idea of where the school will go in the next hundred years. But Dr. Payne has already displayed both strength of purpose and concern for the individual. She is clearly preparing the school in the closing decade of the 20th century to face the challenges of the twenty-first.

Chapter Ten

The Role of the Independent Boarding School

This is perhaps an appropriate point at which to consider some of the most common reasons why parents choose an independent, single-sex boarding school for their children—and why Malvern Girls' College has particular appeal.

For many parents a boarding school offers the chance to provide for their children a stability which they themselves are not able to give, due to the peripatetic life-style imposed upon them by certain types of employment, such as being in the armed forces or in commercial companies which require their staff to travel widely or frequently. In these cases, the need is often recognised, too, by the employer, who will help with the payment of fees or expensive airfares at the beginning and end of term. The state offers very little in the nature of boarding education for this group, so those who point the finger at the social divisions undeniably encouraged by the independent school should perhaps give higher priority to the provision of genuine educational alternatives for the children of such families.

There are other families who are able to solve, for example, the problem of a broken home or an inability or reluctance to take full-time responsibility for the upbringing of their children by paying professionals to do this for extended periods. To the family preoccupied or burdened with the needs of a handicapped child or parent, boarding schools also have much to offer: they enable a child to develop without being swamped by domestic worry. Many other parents greatly value the opportunity presented by the boarding school for a child to develop a spirit of self-reliance and independence. The question 'Why have a child and then send it away for much of the year?'—is easily answered by simple observation of the fact that the child-parent relationship is often enriched by periods of separation which encourage a greater appreciation of each other in the limited time spent together.

Opponents of independent education condemn such opportunities afforded only to those who can pay for them, but they comprise a form of self-help much commended in many cultures which find the notion of a fairy-godmother state unpalatable or frankly impracticable. Supporters of independent education see no reason why they should not be allowed to spend their money in any legal way which appeals to them, and many of the families who buy their children's education have incomes which, although admittedly generally secure, are not particularly high. Elderly relatives and feverishly working parents pay many fees, the costs of which weigh heavily on the consciences of more sensitive pupils. Obviously, for some, the fees are an irritation rather than a real sacrifice and, human nature being what it is, just a few girls are haughtily self-important and self-indulgent, careless of the feelings of others and more ready to take than to give. Such girls are left in no doubt as to what other girls and staff in the school think of them; and is there any school—or society—which does not have its share of unpleasant passengers?

Socially, the most unfortunate reasons for independent education are where the parent opts out of the state system because of real or imagined shortcomings in the state education locally available. In certain regions of the country standards of both discipline and academic attainment have slipped to levels unacceptable to many caring parents, and some choose, sometimes making considerable personal sacrifice to do so, to buy for their children an education not otherwise available to them. Undeniably, this is socially divisive and, in a perfect world, such motivated and usually articulate parents would be devoting their time, talents and money to improving the state system. But in the real world, as every experienced parent knows, lofty principles are the first casualty when the interests of one's own child are at stake. We all want the best we can get for our children, so we try to give our own children any opportunity we were ourselves denied, and we vow to avoid the mistakes our parents made with us. Often happily avoiding these old mistakes, we unwittingly commit our own new ones—but few parents will consciously, for the sake of a better society, sacrifice their own offspring on the altar of their principles of social equality.

Sometimes the shortcomings of the state system are more imagined than real, and occasionally parents make their children unhappy by trying to force them into a social or academic mould which is not appropriate for that particular child. But most pupils respond very positively, happily broadening their circle of friends and developing poise and self-reliance at an earlier age than young people who spend all their time in the family home.

Mindful of the pressures that some parents, usually with the best of intentions, put upon their children, the good independent school is broad in its approach, fostering not only a desire to do well in the academic or sports fields but also a belief in the worth of the individual and any talent which may be used to help the community. In the spirit of the late President Kennedy's exhortation to his fellow Americans, the individual is encouraged to ask not simply what the world owes him or her, but what he or she owes the world. Enjoyment of life is enhanced by a sense of doing something worthwhile: so an important lesson of life in a good independent boarding school is to encourage every pupil to make some contribution, large or small, to the life of the community. This is actually very demanding of staff time and energy and, superficially at least, may have been easier in the old days of the spinster schoolmistress who dedicated her whole life to the school community—often twenty-four hours a day for years at a time. In the modern climate of married teachers with their own domestic responsibilities it is, nevertheless, possible for a boarding school, above all others, to offer facilities and opportunities for all kinds and conditions of adolescents: experts in many fields may be effectively used, often on a part-time basis, both during normal school hours and, perhaps even more significantly, at those times at the weekend and in the evenings when pupils are in their boarding houses. Independent schools have for generations prided themselves on the contribution their pupils make to society: the seed-bed where this is nurtured may be seen as the competition and co-operation between and among the young, aided and abetted by the adults in charge of them seeking to turn a potential problem into a positive advantage to the individual and the community.

Some independent schools, especially those originally founded for boys, have become strongly attached to the principle of co-education but Malvern Girls' College has refused to climb on to this particular bandwagon. There are obvious reasons for the growth of co-education, and some observers find it difficult to believe that there is still a genuine demand for the somewhat artificial segregation of young people on grounds of sex. But such a demand certainly does exist, and some parents choose to send their daughters from co-educational preparatory or primary schools to a girls' school because by the age of about twelve the different rate of development of the adolescent girl from that of the boy is beginning to affect academic progress. Evidence suggests that boys benefit from co-education but girls are more likely to achieve their full potential at single-sex schools.

One undesirable result of co-education did not become apparent until several years' statistics began to build up: it has been shown, in the years since co-education became the more usual method of schooling, that it tends to encourage the notion that scientific subjects are for boys and arts subjects are for girls. In single sex schools there is much less group pressure so that boys feel perfectly normal in entering the Arts Sixth Form and girls in entering on the scientific side. It would seem that if we are to become a society which is truly not sexist there is, ironically, some value in adopting sexual segregation for at least part of the education process! Whilst some would argue that it is more natural for boys and girls to be educated together some parents—and, indeed, some girls—prefer some degree of freedom from emotional pressures which co-education is believed by them to cause. These emotional pressures are not just the overtly sexual, but include also the stresses of contributing in class discussion—difficult enough for many young people in a small class and an insurmountable hurdle for some in large classes with extroverts of the opposite sex.

At the Sixth Form level the single sex girls' school runs some risk of losing pupils who leave to attend boys' schools which accept girls only for Advanced level work. At Malvern these losses are compensated for by the greater number who join the school, often for the benefits perceived to be on offer in a school attended only by girls and staffed largely by women. These benefits are considerable, for the pupil of 16-18 is no longer a child, and some appreciation of the problems of young women is usually more apparent in a girls' school than in many boys' schools which, while paying lip-service to the idea of sexual equality, actually employ only a few token women in assistant rather than senior capacities, and imagine that building a couple of lavatories and putting a netball lesson or two on the timetable constitutes equality. Malvern Girls' College has been particularly successful in coping with the specific problems of sexual equality: whilst the head and most staff are currently female, a good sprinkling of men teaching throughout the school ensures that the male of the species is not rendered more attractive by its rarity value. No particular policy of positive sexual discrimination is apparent either: some heads of department happen to be male and some female—a situation rare in co-educational schools where the top jobs are far more likely to go to men.

The last 25 years have seen enormous changes in education, with a bumper crop of changes occurring in the most recent years. But even in the 1960s, much change was the result of a genuine desire to provide equal opportunities for all and to abolish the branding of a large section of the community as failures because they did not go to a grammar school or failed to reap a respectable harvest of 'O' levels. Malvern Girls' College at that time was very careful not to allow its pupils to be branded as failures and actually accepted a number of girls who had failed their eleven-plus examination, seeing them as having qualities and talents other than academic. Many of them in fact went on to academic success at universities, some following a good degree with further research. So much for the eleven-plus!

Some educational changes made parents uneasy and led to a backlash which has encouraged rather than broken the appeal of independent schooling with its emphasis on old-fashioned values: discipline, hard work and self control. In the 1960s Malvern was economically grateful for, and culturally enriched by, the increased numbers of foreign girls who came here; by the 1980s foreign governments made it increasingly difficult for their subjects to send money out of the country to buy British schooling for their children. So now those places in schools like Malvern are once more being filled by girls whose parents have a jaundiced view of the brave new world of the comprehensive co-educational school, and are willing to pay for traditional rather than trendy approaches to learning. A school which survives as long as Malvern Girls' College has to have a good share of luck, but it also has to be resilient and adaptable, providing what parents want. Whatever fancy names may be given to independent education it is, first and last, a business enterprise which, if it is to achieve commercial success, must respond to market demand. Few girls' schools enjoy the endowments of the ancient public schools founded for boys. Relying entirely on their fees to keep them going, they need to be even more conscious than such boys' schools of what parents are looking for. Parents are their customers and they can never afford to forget it. A large measure of the success enjoyed by Malvern Girls' College is due to the wisdom of those controlling it: they moved with the times. One of the comments made most frequently by former pupils—across several generations—is how liberal, progressive or forward-thinking the school seemed to be. This was the key to its continuing success: it satisfied its customers, adapting itself to meet their needs. Indeed, with their vision of the young woman of the future it might even be claimed that Miss Poulton and Miss Greenslade enjoyed some gift of prophecy as to what their customers would be needing in the years to come: when the demand came, they were certainly well prepared.

Some independent schools fail. Some do so conspicuously by collapsing financially. Others fail their pupils but manage to keep going for a few years. Harsh though the judgement may seem, there is far less excuse for a fee-paying school to fail its pupils than for a state maintained school to do so. Those anxious to proclaim the superiority of the fee-paying school often point to more able teachers and other strange phenomena which they have decided make these schools 'better'. Such prejudiced and ill-informed pronouncements can do serious dis-service to the independent school, carrying with them unpleasantly snobbish assumptions which alienate all right minded people. There is nothing intrinsically better—or worse—about a teacher who happens to earn a living in an independent school rather than a state maintained one. But the pupil to teacher ratio is often better in independent schools and this is an obvious advantage, allowing more individual attention to each pupil.

Independent schools also have two other advantages over the maintained schools. Firstly, they can more easily choose which pupils—and staff—they are prepared to keep within their community. No parent is obliged to send his or her child to a fee-paying school and no such school is obliged to retain an unco-operative pupil, though no school likes to use the ultimate punishment of expulsion. Indeed, there is now reluctance to use even the word 'expulsion', the term 'exclusion' having been adopted instead. But the possibility of exclusion reduces dis-cipline problems dramatically, and a further major reduction is achieved by the marked desire of almost every paying parent to get value for money. Some parents still choose an independent school because of its reputation for good discipline—some have even been known to abdicate their own responsibilities and happily leave the school to impose what they may actually consider to be deserved punishment. If a pupil is so uncooperative as to be suspended or excluded this is seen not simply as a disgrace, but as a waste of hard-earned money, so the children of fee-paying parents, anxious to avoid parental wrath, are likely to be much more amenable to discipline than those whose education is a less obvious drain on parental pockets. Pupils at Malvern Girls' College have sometimes actually voiced the view that any punishment is preferable to informing their parents that they have misbehaved! When a school enjoys such parental backing in the matter of discipline it can turn its attention to the real business of education—making the best of each pupil's talents in a calm and happy atmosphere where staff and pupils are usually on the same side.

The other huge advantage enjoyed by the independent school is its ability to manage its own finances—a power still enjoyed by only a minority of state funded schools. It may increase fees, so long as it is mindful of what the market will stand, in order to provide better facilities. If it allows expenditure to run wild, so that parents no longer consider they are getting value for money, it will lose pupils—its customers—and may collapse. But if it gets its market research right, providing the facilities that parents want at a price they can afford, it steals a march over its competitors in both the state and private sectors. It was the recognition by the Conservative government of the effects of customer demand which led to its encouragement to state schools to 'opt out' of local authority control, leaving schools to manage their own finances. In the case of Malvern Girls' College, finances are managed by its governing Council, whose members give freely of their time, receiving no remuneration. The Council has for decades recognised the need to establish specific committees to deal with a wide variety of matters, some like fees, salaries and maintenance of buildings, needing immediate decisions. Other decisions involve long-term objectives and a Development Committee has now been set up to consider these. Such control and policy planning is vital in today's competitive world and explains the decision in 1990 to appoint a full-time development director.

Chapter Eleven
Reflections on the Past and Looking to the Future

School histories help to satisfy the almost universal desire to reminisce—Do you remember...? Whatever happened to ... ? Fancy that still being there! At some point all pupils become former pupils and Malvern Girls' College's flourishing Old Girls' Association indicates that large numbers still feel an interest in and affection for the place which figured so prominently during their formative years. The school has to thank this association for much that it has done in both intangible ways and in material gifts, such as the provision of the apron stage in the York Hall in 1954, refurbishment of the chapel and the establishment of bursaries and scholarships. The desire of so many girls to retain some links with their old school must mean that they feel some sense of gratitude for what their education here gave them. Some show this in a very positive way by sending their daughters here. Further proof that many girls, parents and staff feel gratitude for what the school offers is afforded by the formation in 1975 of the group known as the Friends of Malvern Girls' College, which continues to act as a focus for social contact and fund-raising to put the icing on the cake of facilities which the school offers.

The school historian's task is not easy because people have very different ideas on what a school history should contain and it is impossible to please everyone. Why do schools want their history written down? Presumably because at certain points in their development a need is felt to look back to see what has been achieved and remind the present generation how much effort that involved; and perhaps there is also an unspoken hope that it will provide some pointers to the future. This means asking several questions: What does the school stand for? What is a good education? Where are we going in the next hundred years?

What does an education at Malvern Girls' College mean? Since education should instill knowledge, skills and values to equip pupils for life, it is very pertinent to ask what pupils do after they leave school. The answer to this question gives important clues as to how well a school has served both its pupils and the community at large. But it is impossible to answer in great detail, for all schools lose touch with many of their former pupils with the result that any conclusions to be drawn must be based on evidence from only part of the total pupil population. There are, however, some valid deductions to be made even from this incomplete evidence. Malvern Girls' College has retained links with several thousand of its pupils over the years in a variety of ways including its Old Girls' Association. So what can we learn about the contribution made by this school to the wider community at home and abroad?

Since it is a girls' school with a hundred years of history it naturally reflects in microcosm the changing attitudes to girls' education and the changing status of women over that period. When it was founded women had neither the vote nor equal pay in those few careers open to them. Women have come a long way since then. The limitations placed on women did not stop the school's founders from building up a highly successful business. That business was successful not simply because it satisfied the requirements of parents who wanted to turn out accomplished daughters, but also because it moved with—or even ahead of—the times: it equipped girls for a fulfilled life independent of men—fathers, brothers or husbands—if they chose or if, as was the sad case for many women after the Great War, it was thrust upon them.

The effort to get Doris Moss to Somerville College, Oxford, in 1912 points not only to her academic promise, but also to the school's ambition: to claim such an achievement for one of its pupils would bathe the school in glory, for at that time very few university places were available for women, and neither Oxford nor Cambridge was yet prepared actually to confer a degree on a woman. By 1939 Miss Brooks was boasting at Prize Giving of 31 university scholarships and exhibitions won by girls over a period of five years. In 1946 she announced that, since the first scholarship to Oxford won in 1921, the college had notched up a total of 95 scholarships including 40 to Oxford, 28 to Cambridge and three to London. The school was justifiably proud of its academic standards, which were maintained even during the difficulties of the Second World War: in those six years of war, 76 university places were won in competition with schools throughout the country, and 42 scholarships were achieved.

Osra Garrish, indefatigable secretary of the Old Girls' Association for many years, produced in 1947 a fascinating analysis of the occupations of members. As is always the case with women, large numbers did little to advance the feminist cause, modestly dismissing themselves as 'only a housewife'. Others gave more specific clues so that the following information could be compiled to indicate the wide range of work undertaken by old girls, significant numbers having joined the forces during the war:

55 in the W.R.N.S.	2 magistrates
55 in the A.T.S.	3 solicitors
37 in the W.A.A.F.	5 architects
26 in other war-related capacities	1 estate agent
	3 librarians
17 doctors	19 administrative civil servants
65 nurses	2 B.B.C. announcers
15 physiotherapists	5 in banks
5 speech therapists	10 in dramatic art
3 radiographers	3 company directors
7 hospital almoners	9 scientists (including research)
60 teachers	17 in agriculture and horticulture
66 secretaries	2 writers

8 in domestic science and household management
82 students at universities and training colleges

In addition, countless members were doing youth work with guides, cubs and other organisations; other posts included editorial assistants, reporters and musicians. The perennial plea of the secretary for more news of more members suggests that this list is far from complete, and yet shows that the college was making a very real impact in professional and vocational work.

With subtle changes, this impact has continued since that analysis was made. In preparation for the writing of this centenary history, a questionnaire was sent to each of the 3,000 members of the Old Girls Association. Their replies showed a wide diversity of life-styles and achievements but through this rich tapestry ran threads which reflected, whatever their circumstances, the impact of their education: care for others, high standards and a willingness to work hard towards a worthwhile goal in both personal and professional lives. Their answers illustrated that the school's achievement does not lie simply in turning out women who reach the top of all kinds of professional trees, important and gratifying though it is for the school to have produced the first woman high court judge, the first woman in the stock exchange or the first woman elected to the Council of the Institute of Civil Engineers. The school does even more than that: it turns out women who can, through attitude and dedication, influence society and gently change it to recognise the contribution that anyone, man or woman, can make to it. Because many girls originate from, or go to work in, foreign countries this influence is world wide, so Britain continues to make an impact outside its own shores, long after the demise of its empire.

This is perhaps the most important feature of education to a woman: to have the true strength, confidence and self-value to be a man's equal without turning feminism into a piece of artillery which reduces men to occupying the inferior position they once accorded women. Probably the main achievement of the first hundred years of Malvern Girls' College has been its contribution to a changed perception of women's place in society, a role which is very different from that of the 19th century when our story began.

The Latin of the school motto pays no attention to gender. *Vincit qui se vincit* means *He/ She conquers who first conquers him/herself*. If self-conquest is the precursor of success the conquest is more assured if education enables both boys and girls to acquire self-knowledge.

Postscript

As this book was going to press, exciting new developments were announced for Centenary Year: a restructuring of boarding arrangements for the Middle School, including additional computer facilities, coupled with major changes in the use of the Founders' Library in the main building.

Middle School boarding houses have traditionally taken pupils aged 11 to 16, but now Ivydene Hall and Summerside will be extensively refurbished to provide specifically for the needs of younger girls in Upper Three and Lower Four, while the other Middle School houses will look after Upper Fourth, Lower Fifth and Upper Fifth form girls.

This break with tradition will provide greater privacy in more comfortable houses and shows the school facing the latest challenge to boarding schools at the end of the 20th century. Improvements in information services and better technology will enable girls to work more independently and efficiently, and ensure that they will be much better equipped to face the challenges which confront modern women.

The announcement is, indeed, a promising start to our second century!

Appendix A

Principals and Headmistresses

Principals

1893	Miss Isabel Greenslade
	Miss Lily S. Poulton
1899	Miss Blanche E. Mitchell
1912	Miss Kate Dawson

Headmistresses

1919	Miss Kate Dawson
1928	Miss Iris M. Brooks
1954	Miss Margaret M. Burgess
1968	Miss Veronica M. H. Owen
1984	Mrs. Eileen Stamers-Smith
1985	Miss C. Delmé Moore
1986	Dr. Valerie B. Payne

Chairmen of the College Council

1933	Sir Anderson Montague Barlow P.C.
1946	Lady Atkins
1950	H. H. Hardy C.B.E.
1956	Sir Geoffrey Winterbotham
1964	Mrs. Arthur Gibbs
1968	T. A. Hamilton Baynes O.B.E.
1972	Prof. B. N. Brooke M.D., M.Chir.
1982	J. W. G. Frith B.A., F.C.A.

Appendix C

Staff in 1955

STAFF

Vice-Mistress:	Miss D. M. Puttock, Hon. Mods. (Oxon.)
Senior Mistress:	Miss E. M. Foster, m.a. (Oxon.)
Headmistress's Secretary:	Mrs H. Pudsey
Asst. Secretaries:	Miss C. M. Kjeldsen, Miss J. Share.
Assistant Bursar:	Miss E. G. Young, a.a.c.c.a.
Domestic Bursar:	*Miss G. W. Phillips, Diploma of the Bedford Physical Training College, C.S.P.
Medical Officer of Health:	Dr Stella Macdonald, m.r.c.s., l.r.c.p.
Sanatorium:	Sister W. M. Mercer, s.r.n.

English:	*Miss D. M. G. Danne (Librarian), b.a. (Bristol), a.lib.a.
	*Miss E. M. Foster, m.a. (Oxon.)
	Miss E. G. Yelland, b.a. (Exeter)
History:	Mrs Benson Davies (also Geography), b.a. (Cantab.)
	Mrs M. M. Moreton (also Scripture), b.a., d.th.p.t. (Durham)
Geography:	Miss J. Roberts (Careers Mistress), b.sc., a.k.c. (Lond.)
Scripture:	Rev. R. B. Lunt, m.a. (Oxon.)
	Miss J. Williams (also History, Latin), b.a. (Durham)
Classics:	Miss J. M. Oakley, b.a. (Lond.)
	*Miss W. M. Warry, b.a. (Lond.)
	†Miss M. Williams, b.a. (Lond.)
French:	Miss S. Berry, b.a. (Manch.)
	*Miss J. Jones, b.a. (Leeds)
	*Miss M. Tamplin, b.a. (Oxon.)
French and German:	Miss J. Kirkman, b.a. (Oxon.)
German:	Miss G. Horowitz, Vienna University
Spanish and Italian:	Miss M. L. Watkins, Diplômée (Rennes)
Mathematics:	Miss P. Z. Bennett, b.sc. (Bristol)
	Miss D. M. Puttock, Hon. Mods. (Oxon.)
	Miss A. E. Sharp, b.a. (Cantab.)
	Miss K. S. Yates (also Physics), b.sc. (Lond.)
Natural Sciences:	†Miss B. Handley, b.sc. (Lond.) *Physics*
	Miss M. Jago, b.sc. (Lond.) *Zoology*
	Miss M. E. John, m.sc. (Lond.) *Chemistry*
	*Miss M. M. Micklewright, b.sc. (Lond.) *Botany*
	Miss M. Waters, b.sc. (Lond.) *Botany*
Domestic Science:	Miss J. Roundhill, Berridge House T. Cert. Dom. Sc.
Art and Crafts:	Miss P. M. Knowler, a.t. Dipl.
	Miss J. F. Mayne, a.t. Dipl.
Speech Training:	Miss J. H. Cowell, Teach. Dipl., Dipl. Dram. Art.
	Miss M. B. Evans, Teach. Dipl., Dipl. Dram. Art.
Secretarial Subjects:	†Miss M. J. Hall, Kerr-Sander Sec. Dipl.

Gymnastics and Games:	Miss C. A. Martineau, Diploma of the Dartford College of Physical Education, Lond. Dipl. in Physical Education
	Miss F. Shipley, Diploma of the Bedford Physical Training College, C.S.P.
	Miss S. W. Wood, Diploma of Anstey College of Physical Education, Cert. of Education of Birmingham University
	Mrs Scott-Bowden (Hockey Coach)
Tennis:	The Dewpool School of Lawn Tennis Coaching
Dancing:	Miss B. Davies, m.b.b.o., m.o.d.s.t., Inter. and Full Teaching Diploma

Music Department

Head of Department—Piano and Singing: †Miss E. Jackman, l.r.a.m.

Piano:	Miss J. Barker, a.r.m.c.m.
	Miss M. Bowyer, a.r.c.m., g.r.s.m.
	Miss J. Coats, l.r.a.m.
	Miss R. H. Margetts, l.r.a.m., a.r.c.m.
	Miss M. I. McKee, l.r.a.m.
Piano, Flute, Singing:	Miss B. T. Rodd, a.r.c.m., g.r.s.m.
Piano and Oboe:	Miss M. Clarke, l.r.a.m.
Piano and Clarinet:	Miss S. Spyers, l.r.a.m., a.r.c.m.
Piano and Organ:	Miss M. Kemp, l.r.a.m.
Violin and Viola:	Miss M. Martindale-Taylor, a.r.c.m.
Violoncello and Double Bass:	Miss M. Edes, m.i.s.m., Solo Performer
Piano, Harmony, and Theory of Music:	Miss A. Bushby, l.r.a.m.

Junior School (Hatley St. George)

Mistress-in-Charge:	Miss M. V. M. Cayley, Ass. Inst. Ling. (French)
	Miss J. W. Dennis, M. of Ed. Teacher's Certificate
	Mrs E. E. Douglas, b.a. (Durham)
	Miss C. P. McCoy, b.a. (Lond.)
	Miss E. H. Travess, M. of Ed. Teacher's Certificate

Preparatory School (Parkfield)

Mistress-in-Charge:	Miss E. A. Temperley, N.F.U. Certificate.
	Miss D. W. Beale, N.F.F. Certificate
	Miss N. M. Murray, N.F.F. Certificate
	Miss J. Norton, M. of Ed. Teacher's Certificate

*Housemistress of Middle School Houses.
†Landing Mistresses in Senior House.

Some Key Dates in the History of the College Buildings

1893	School opened at Ivydene, College Road
1899	Purchase of Ivydene Hall (Montpellier) with one acre
1903	Purchase of Summerside
1905	Ryall House rented for staff and sanatorium. Bought 1931
1908	The Mount taken for Juniors
1910	Purchase of main playing field
1911	First laboratory
1913	The Benhams bought and enlarged as Senior House
1915	Lindfield rented for Domestic Science. Bought 1954
	Abbotsmead rented for the founders
1917	Hatley St George rented for preparatory department
	Purchase of Avenue House. Chantry rented as overflow for Hatley St George
1919	Beaufort rented for preparatory department
	Purchase of *Imperial Hotel* and baths
1920	Gymnasium, with Swedish apparatus at Avenue. Grattanhurst rented
1921	Orchard Lodge, Standish Lodge, Joyfield and Freshford bought
1922	Abbotsmead bought and enlarged by founders
1922-23	Gallery added to assembly hall in main building
1925	Purchase of golf course and house by Miss Greenslade
1925	School corridor adapted for library
1927-28	Main building extended
1929	Laboratories extended
1929	Goodrest (staff house) and Woodgate (sanatorium) bought
1934	New wing built—York Hall, Founders' Library, cloakrooms
1939	New Benhams opened
1939	Houses bought/rented for evacuation
1946	Batsford bought (bursar's flat in 1954)
1952	Top of tower removed
1956-59	Biology block built
1959	Chapel refurbished
1963	Hatfield built
1967	Swimming baths improved
1971	Fireproof doors began to appear on stair-cases and corridors
1978	Edinburgh Dome opened
1988	Greenslade opened as new Senior House
	Senior House refurbished and renamed Poulton
1989	All weather pitches
1991	Computer suite opened in Room D

Malvern Girls' College School Song

Through the days of youth you are often told
That you are young and the world is old.
Remember the old world's heart is young
And, whenever the old new song is sung,
Carry on with heart and mind and soul
Straight on until you reach the goal.

Chorus
Though you win or lose, succeed or fail,
Let your eye not dim nor your spirit quail.
Let your heart be light and your arm be strong
As you go through the world to the lilt of the song.
Carry on! Carry on!

Oh, you who are older and look from afar,
What your schooldays were our schooldays are;
Remember that once you too were young,
Light of heart and strong of lung;
And firm as a rock the building stood,
When each man worked for the next man's good.

Chorus

Carry on though the game be hard and long,
Do the right thing and scorn the wrong.
Men look to you to lead the way,
With a smile on your lips through the roughest day.
See that the School still keeps her name,
Be strong of purpose—play the game.

Chorus

Carry on when you come, and when you go
Carry on to a tune not sad nor slow.
And though you find life scarce the same
As when you played your youthful game,
The goal is still before your eyes
The straightest course shall win the prize.

Chorus

These words were written by Ella Stratton (at school 1914 -17). She qualified as a doctor in 1923.
Music was composed by Muriel Cross (at school 1918 -21). She went to the Royal Academy of Music in 1921
and became a professional musician known as Judy Hoade.

The song has not been sung for many years.

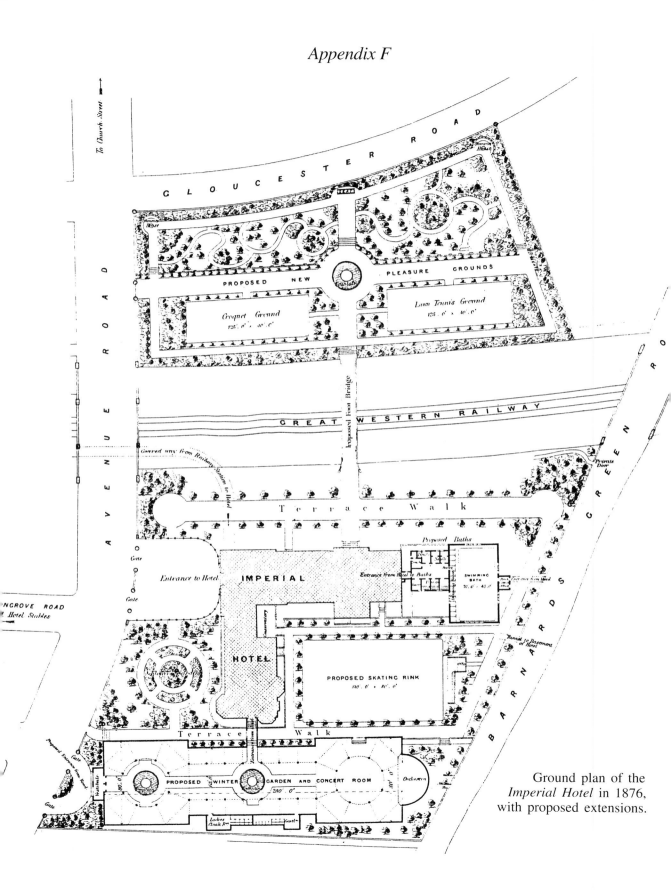

Ground plan of the
Imperial Hotel in 1876,
with proposed extensions.

Bibliography

Primary sources:
Foley Estate Sale Catalogue, 1910
Imperial Hotel Guide, 1875
Imperial Hotel Guide, early 20th century

Clothes lists
Deeds of school property
Letters from school to parents
Letters from parents and ex-pupils
School Magazines
Malvern Gazette and Ledbury Reporter
Malvern Illustrated 1894
Malvern News
Matrons' books
Minutes of meetings of governing body
Oral and written recollections of Old Girls and staff
Phillips, Grace W., *Smile, Bow and Pass On*, 1980
School prospectuses

Secondary sources and further reading:
Avery, Gillian, *The Best Type of Girl,* 1991
Blumenau, Ralph A., *History of Malvern College*, 1965
Burley, Rosa, *Edward Elgar:the Record of a Friendship*
Barnard, H. C., *A History of English Education from 1760*, 1963
Curtis, S. J., *History of Education in Great Britain*, 1968
Curtis, S. J., and Boultwood, M. E. A., *History of English Education since 1800*, 1966
Faithfull, Lilian M., *In the House of my Pilgrimage*, 1924
Gardiner, Dorothy, *English Girlhood at School*, 1929
Gaunt, H. C. A., *Two Exiles*, 1946
Goodman, Jean, *Anything but Housework*, 1973
Haddon, Celia, *Great Days and Jolly Days*, 1977
Hurle, Pamela, *Bygone Malvern*, 1989
Hurle, Pamela, *The Malvern Hills*, 1984
Hurle, Pamela, *The Malverns*, 1992
Hurle, Pamela, and Winsor, John, *Portrait of Malvern*, 1985
Magnus, Laurie, *The Jubilee Book of the Girls' Public Day School Trust, 1873-1923*, 1923
Percival, Alicia C., *The English Miss Today and Yesterday*, 1939
Seaborne, Malcolm, *The English School, Its Architecture and Organisation 1370-1870*, 1971
Walford, Geoffrey (ed.), *British Public Schools: Policy and Practice*, 1984

Index